THE HISTORY

OF THE

BRITISH FILM

1896–1906

by

RACHAEL LOW

and

ROGER MANVELL

Based upon research of the History Committee
of the BRITISH FILM INSTITUTE
Chairman: Cecil Hepworth

LONDON

GEORGE ALLEN & UNWIN LTD

FIRST PUBLISHED IN 1948

PRINTED IN GREAT BRITAIN
in 11-point Plantin type
BY UNWIN BROTHERS LIMITED
LONDON AND WOKING

THE HISTORY OF THE
BRITISH FILM

1896–1906

Further volumes of *The History of the British Film*
covering the periods 1906–1914 and 1914–1928
are in preparation

In 1946, fifty years after the appearance in Great Britain of the cinema as a regular form of public entertainment, the British Film Institute set up a Research Committee to initiate and guide research into the authentic history of the British cinema both as an art and as an industry. In order to make the results of the Committee's work public as soon as possible, it has been decided to publish the history period by period, 1896–1906 being the first. The personnel of this advisory committee, under the chairmanship of the veteran film producer Mr. Cecil Hepworth, consisted of Mr. George Pearson, the producer; Mr. Ernest Lindgren, the Curator of the National Film Library; Dr. Roger Manvell; and Miss Rachael Low. The Committee is grateful to Dr. Manvell and to Miss Low for initiating the scheme and for planning the necessary research.

Miss Low has interviewed a large number of pioneers in all aspects of the development of the British film, has collected documents, catalogues, periodicals, and photographs of the period under review and has been responsible for writing and compiling the text of this book. As a result of an appeal through the Press and also through many private channels in the industry a considerable body of material has been assembled, comprising such items as catalogues, contemporary publicity and press reviews, private notes, letters and memoirs, stills and photographs. Special thanks are due to Mr. F. W. Baker, Mr. R. H. Cricks, Mr. W. Fearn, Mr. T. France, Mr. G. A. Smith, Mr. E. G. Turner, and Major T. Williamson.

The Committee's terms of reference did not include research into the invention or later history of cinematograph apparatus, for which some body such as the Science Museum[1] is better fitted. Reference to technical developments has therefore only been made incidentally, and where such developments are inextricable from the other aspects of the story. A brief statement of some well-known claims and records of early demonstrations of screen projection in this country has been included in an Appendix, as of general interest. This is not intended, however, to be the last word on a

[1] The Science Museum in South Kensington has an extensive collection of early apparatus.

subject which is extremely controversial and must ultimately receive separate treatment.

It should be emphasized that this work is intended primarily as a reference book, a brief summary of the findings of some badly needed research, and if the inclusion of producers' synopses makes entertaining reading in the latter part, this should not obscure the value of the earlier chapters. The plain facts there presented were already tangled and obscured when research began, and to sift and assemble them in a simple record was the central task of the Committee. As with all research, new facts are continually coming to light, and even the present delays in publication have made some revision necessary. Such revision can be continued indefinitely but it is necessary to draw the line somewhere and publish the material as it stands, with the hope that any further alterations needed can be incorporated in a second edition.

CONTENTS

APPENDICES

ILLUSTRATIONS

INSET ONE

between pages 32 and 33

INSET TWO

between pages 80 and 81

PART ONE

PRODUCTION, DISTRIBUTION AND EXHIBITION

CHAPTER ONE

Principal Film Producers before 1906

THE PRODUCERS

The transformation of the motion picture from a toy or a curiosity discussed at scientific and photographic societies into a major industry, a young art and an educational force started when it became a regular commercial form of entertainment. In the half-century since the first audience paid to see a moving picture show an entirely new industry has sprung up to fill an important place in the national economy. A new art form appealing to one of the widest publics any art has ever known, has forced its way to a position of cultural importance despite the hostility of many devotees of the older arts. Led by artists, intellectuals, pioneering spirits with inspired faith in its possibilites; debased by the cynics, the commercially minded, and the socially irresponsible—in the hands of an uneasy and unwieldy fusion of artists, technicians and businessmen, parasites and creative workers—the youngest art has developed in all directions, good as well as bad. At the same time, undifferentiated and unintended, one of the most powerful means for influencing public opinion has formed itself in the hands of this same chance agglomeration of adventurers, crusaders and craftsmen. Even the educational and instructional film and the documentary, films with a deliberate and responsible social purpose, have their origins in the same burst of undiscriminating enterprise which characterizes the first ten years of the commercial film.

The dozen or so companies which produced films in this period show a typical pattern of development which is in most cases the story of one man of exceptional versatility and initiative. As might be expected, many of the pioneer producers came to cinematography through photography or the optical lantern—Birt Acres, James Bamforth, Esme Collings, Cecil

Hepworth, Frank Mottershaw, G. A. Smith and James Williamson had all been connected professionally with one or the other. Becoming interested in the projection of motion pictures, in most cases as a novelty to add to their own lantern lectures, they were faced with the difficulty of buying apparatus and films, especially the latter. Being the type of men they were, they proceeded to make their own—not only their own films, but in many cases their own apparatus as well. Small companies sprang up all over the country in the last four years of the nineteenth century— in Yorkshire, Lancashire, Sheffield, London, and Brighton. Almost every firm was dominated by one man, who devised his own equipment and methods: wrote, produced, and as often as not acted (with members of his family) in his own films: and marketed and sometimes exhibited them himself. In most cases he also sold cinematograph equipment, as well as taking films to customers' orders, and carrying on an extensive export business.

This combination of inventor, artist, business man and showman was possible because of the elementary methods used in production. Actuality and topical films (see pages 51 and 61) and even simple "made-up"[1] films needed even less preparation than amateur theatricals. But as films became longer and more elaborate, professional actors were employed, indoor studios came into use, and technical equipment became more complex. Cinematography was becoming increasingly specialized, and those producers who either could not, or would not, make the transition from semi-amateur Jack-of-all-trades to full professional status gradually dropped away.

This process had hardly begun in the period covered in this survey. In 1906 R. W. Paul, who was to retire from cinematography about 1910, was still one of the most popular producers in this country. Travelling showmen up and down the country were producing their own films, and not only "locals" (i.e. films of local scenes or events to arouse special interest in the audience) but stories as well. Walter Haggar, one of these travelling showmen, is included in the present chapter as an outstanding example of this type of producer. This has been possible because his films were circulated widely through Gaumont. Many other showmen, because they had no regular channels of distribution, have left little trace. If only for

[1] The term is Hepworth's. See lecture to the B.K.S., February 3, 1936.

this reason, therefore, the following list of producers cannot claim to be comprehensive. It contains brief biographical sketches of each of the more important concerns and representative examples of the smaller companies. But it should be remembered that even in 1906 anyone with the ingenuity to devise or adapt the elementary apparatus needed, and film a few hundred feet of "phantom ride," comic scene or news event, could claim to be a film producer.[1]

Autoscope Company

William George Barker, later to become one of the most famous and spectacular of British films producers, began film production as an amateur in 1896. For a few years his film activities consisted of showing his own films at occasional free film shows, and it was not until 1901 that he became a professional. In this year he founded the Autoscope Company (50, Gray's Inn Road), and towards the end of the same year erected an open-air stage at Stamford Hill. This, a very elementary affair, consisted of two scaffold poles and a drop roll canvas background borrowed from Stoke Newington Theatre. It was erected in the Running Grounds at Stamford Hill, for which privilege Barker paid £5 a year in rent and gave free shows from time to time. This modest arrangement was superseded in 1904 by the famous studio at Ealing (see p. 32), which for years was one of the largest and most up-to-date studios in this country.

Barker, who subsequently became famous for his lavish dramatic productions, was at this time chiefly known for his concentration on topical subjects. Towards the end of the period under review, he became Managing Director of the Warwick Trading Company (see p. 27), by which the Autoscope Company was absorbed.

Bamforth & Company, Ltd.

James Bamforth of Station Road, Holmfirth, Yorkshire, was one of the smaller producers who for some time existed on equal terms with the larger concerns.

Originally fairly important dealers in lantern slides and picture postcards, Bamforth's did not take up cinematography until 1899 or 1900, when they

[1] See p. 28 for sources used in this chapter.

teamed up with Riley Brothers of Bradford,[1] who were the proud possessors of a camera. They produced a number of films, mainly broad farce, for which they hired local talent. With these films, their representatives toured the North of England.

Compared with the larger companies they produced few films, and although they did export a little to the Continent in later years, their fame was mainly local. Nevertheless, in the days when ingenuity counted for more than specialized equipment and elaborate organization, there is no reason to believe that the films of such companies as Bamforth's were in any way inferior to much of the output of larger and more important firms.

British Mutoscope & Biograph Company

The British Mutoscope & Biograph Company is of particular interest in that it, with MaGuire and Baucus (see p. 25), is one of the first two film companies in Britain that started as branches of American companies. Unlike MaGuire and Baucus, the British Mutoscope and Biograph Company retained this character. Its Managing Director and moving spirit from its inception in 1897 was an American, E. B. Koopman, one of the members of the parent company, the American Mutoscope and Biograph Company. The studio built by the Biograph Company behind the Tivoli (see p. 30) was erected almost at once, and seems to have been one of the earliest in the world.

The financial interests of the company were considered large at the time, as indeed they were in comparison with the amateurish one-man concerns which were the current form of film manufacture. However, the fact that its interests included the Mutoscope penny-in-the-slot machines as well as cinematography places it in a special category. The company was not at first a rival to other producing firms in the usual sense, as it made films for a large-gauge machine of its own, and neither were sold to free-lance operators. They were exhibited chiefly in music-halls, and ran a show for several years at the Palace Theatre in London. These films entered the ordinary market by about 1900, but did not achieve the world-wide fame and popularity of American Biograph films. Exclusive rights in England to all Biograph films, including American and German, were held by Gaumont by 1904.

[1] Riley Brothers, 55-7, Goodwin St., lantern equipment manufacturers.

Charles Urban Trading Company

Charles Urban founded this company when he broke away from the Warwick Trading Company (see p. 25) early in 1903. He himself was a business man and *entrepreneur* rather than a producer, consequently a greater number of films are connected with his name than with that of any other film pioneer in this country, although he himself was not directly responsible for them. It was to his initiative and remarkable grasp of the film's potentialities that the early British film industry owes such ambitious achievements as the scientific film, Kinemacolor, and the travel and war films of first the Warwick Trading Company and then the Charles Urban Trading Company—films which are outstanding in comparison with their contemporaries. Many of the photographers who made the W.T.C. what it was under Urban left it when he did and continued to work for him in his new company.[1] In 1903 the operators of the C.U.T.C. made about 250 films, and this quantity was greatly exceeded in the next three years.

The foremost of Urban's cameramen was Joe Rosenthal. No. 1037 in Urban's catalogue (i.e. either May or June, 1903—the earliest months of this company's career) begins a travel series taken by Rosenthal called *Living Canada*. March 1904 found him in Switzerland with Ormiston-Smith and Lansdorff, making the *Winter Sports Series*. He came into his own as a war camera-man during the Russo-Japanese War, starting with a series of strongly pro-Japanese behind-the-lines films, of which *Home Life of the Jolly Jap* is a typically significant title. For a while nothing more exciting appeared, but the C.U.T.C. was making much of the fact that Rosenthal was present at the siege of Port Arthur [2] and would be sending home a magnificent series of action pictures as soon as circumstances permitted. In the meantime they did their best with a "Wonderful Representation of the Bombardment of Port Arthur" supplied by West's "Our Navy" Ltd. Rosenthal's pictures of the real siege, the most spectacular series of war films so far seen, finally reached England and were first shown privately at the Japanese Legation on April 20, 1905.

F. Ormiston-Smith was another who came with Urban from the W.T.C. By the summer of 1903 Urban was announcing a series taken by him called *The Wintry Alps*, and later in the year *Picturesque Switzerland*. In September he led an expedition similar to that previously sponsored by

[1] See p. 25 for Urban's career at the W.T.C.   [2] August 1904 to February 1905.

B

the Warwick Company (see p. 26), and climbed the Jungfrau (September 24, 1903) and the Matterhorn (September 28, 1903). From early spring, 1904, he toured Greece, Turkey, Egypt, Arabia and Palestine, and in February 1905, he went to Sweden to make the *Northern Ice Sports Series*.

Some of the first films marketed by the C.U.T.C. were an Indian series taken by Dr. J. Gregory Mantle. C. Rider Noble was "operating with the Bulgarian Army" in the autumn of 1903, and secured a series of films behind the lines. A few months later he was with the insurgent bands of Macedonia and actually took scenes of the fighting. George Rogers, an American, was one of Urban's agents in the Russo-Japanese War, working with the Russians while Rosenthal worked with the Japanese. Together, they kept the British public remarkably well supplied with films of this struggle. H. M. Lomas led the "Urban Bioscope Expedition through Borneo" in 1903 and through Malay in 1904, making a special series of films for the North Borneo Company. The interesting similarity of this undertaking to the industrial sponsorship of documentary films in later years is mentioned below (see p. 60).

Another field in which Urban films led the way was that of the scientific and instructional film. On August 17, 1903, two important series of films taken by F. Martin Duncan were first shown at the Alhambra Theatre. These were the *Natural History* and the *Unseen World* series, the latter being a remarkable use of the microscope in combination with the motion picture camera. These, with later additions, continued to be shown for years and enjoyed considerable popularity. Press notices of the time show that the educational nature of these films was explicitly recognized by the public, which, far from being deterred by the idea, was greatly attracted.

A lifelong colleague of Urban was G. A. Smith (born 1864), whose inventive genius displayed itself in many important developments of cinematography. A portrait photographer in Brighton, he knew as neighbours the other pioneers who worked in this early film centre—W. Friese-Greene, E. Collings, J. Williamson and A. Darling. Like many others who were later to become producers, he first became interested in films as novel illustrations to his own lectures. This was in 1896, when films were hard to come by, so he devised his own camera and by 1897 had begun to make his own films, simple actualities taken on the beach or in the back garden. He sold his first film on April 13, 1897, and business was so good that by August 1900, he had made £1,800 profit.

During this time he had been experimenting with trick photography, and in 1897 had even taken out a patent for double-exposure, which he first used for the vision in *The Corsican Brothers*. His first trick films preceded those of R. W. Paul by several years, and he even seems to have anticipated much of the work of G. Méliès in France. It is interesting for example, that *Cinderella and the Fairy Godmother* and *Faust and Mephistopheles* were produced not later than September 1898, whereas Méliès' famous *Cendrillon* was not made until 1900, and his *Faust and Marguerite* in 1904. Whoever took the lead in this type of motion picture, it seems certain that Smith, working quietly in the English seaside town, was ahead of the rest of the world in film technique, and even used the interpolated close-up as early as 1900 (see p. 49).

In 1900 Smith ceased production on his own account, and started to work for the Warwick Trading Company, with a two-year contract to print some fifty films (i.e. about 5,000 ft.) per day. In addition, a studio was built for him at St. Anne's Well Garden. His close association with Charles Urban lasted for many more years, and together—Smith as inventor and Urban as *entrepreneur*—they subsequently put the first successful colour system on the market.

Esme Collings

Esme Collings was a well-known Brighton portrait photographer, and one of the very first to take up the production of cinema films, starting in 1896, even before G. A. Smith (according to Smith himself).

The following account is taken from the notebooks of his contemporary and neighbour, James Williamson:

He produced during this year[1] about thirty short-length subjects which are believed to have had a good sale. One at least was of dramatic interest and of good quality. This was probably the first film in which a well-known actor appeared. The film was a scene from *The Broken Melody*, in which Mr. Van Biene himself took the principal part. No further films from this producer were traceable, but he was understood to have carried out a series of costly experiments in film and apparatus of the Biograph size. Mr. Collings announced on his shop front that he was "formerly in partnership with Mr. Friese-Greene."

[1] i.e. 1896.

He seems, however, to have been of local importance only, and to have left little trace. He is of significance merely as a representative of the early amateur cinematographers who failed to make the transition to full professional production.

Clarendon Film Company

This firm, which was comparable in size and importance with Cricks and Sharp or Mitchell and Kenyon, was founded rather late in the period (1904) by H. V. Lawley and Percy Stow, and had a studio at Limes Road, Croydon. Lawley was an early partner of Cecil Hepworth, whom he left in order to found this company. Most of its history belongs to a later period. Clarendon films, which were few, were mainly comics and were distributed from October 1904, through Gaumont. A total order of from thirty to forty copies per subject was a good average for companies of this size.

Cricks and Sharp

G. H. Cricks was employed by George Harrison and Co., Ltd., a firm of stationers, when the latter opened a photographic business towards the end of the century. Cricks, who was an amateur photographer, was put in charge, and produced a number of films.[1] From here he went to Paul's Animatograph Works, where, in 1900, he was made the manager of one of the departments.

About 1901 he left Paul to found Cricks and Sharp, in company with H. M. Sharp. The premises of this company were at London Road, Mitcham, and consisted of a cottage which served for office and laboratory, a greenhouse which was used for another laboratory, and an outdoor stage. A small river ran through the grounds, and was used in many films. Cricks made films of the usual type, with particular success in "comics." Quick to adopt any new developments—the chase film, the close-up, etc.—he was representative of the small producers who were unostentatiously building up the reputation of British films in the years before the First World War.

[1] *Maria Marten or Murder in the Red Barn, East Lynne,* etc.

Gaumont and Company

The Gaumont Company in Britain, a branch of the French concern, was started in September 1898 by A. C. Bromhead and T. A. Welsh, with an office in Cecil Court. At first the business consisted of selling films and equipment from France, but in time Gaumont films were produced in Britain too, and the English office became one of the most important selling agents in the world for both British and foreign films. Lumière, Hepworth, Clarendon, Williamson, Biograph, Mitchell and Kenyon and Norwood films were included in the famous "Elge" monthly lists of films, besides the Gaumont films themselves. Notable among the latter are the faked war films and the productions of Alfred Collins,[1] who was one of the first British directors to adopt the chase film. On an average, this company published some hundred films a year towards the end of the period.

Haggar and Sons

Walter Haggar was a travelling showman, well-known in the fair-grounds, especially in South Wales (see p. 37). Like many other travelling showmen, he had his own camera and made "locals" of either scenic or topical interest (see p. 54). In addition to this, he went in for story production on an ambitious scale. Stories and comic scenes were produced by many of the fair-ground showmen for their own use, but Haggar seems to have been unusual in that his films were widely circulated among other exhibitors all over the world—according to Col. Bromhead, who handled them, 480 prints of *The Salmon Poachers* alone were sold. With his family's help he made films equal in length and elaboration to any of the period. He even reached the comparatively advanced idea of a "series"—the *Mirthful Mary* series. His films were marketed by Gaumont, who held the distribution rights except in South Wales, where they could only be shown by Haggar himself or with permission from him. In comparison with full time producers with studios Haggar produced few films—some three or four a year after about 1902—but these were of a sufficiently high standard to merit distribution on an equal footing with those of the most important firms. His *Life of Charles Peace* was one of the most advanced films of the period.

[1] E.g. *Welshed, a Derby Incident* (see p. 48) and *A Runaway Match* (see p. 47).

Hepworth Manufacturing Company

Cecil Hepworth (born 1874) was the son of a famous lantern lecturer, T. C. Hepworth. He entered the film world in 1896 with the sale to R. W. Paul of six hand-feed electric arc lamps of his own design. After touring the country with his own cinematograph show, Hepworth was engaged by Charles Urban to work for MaGuire Baucus. In 1897 he published what is probably the first handbook of cinematography ever written, which "put in convenient form the salient features of cinematography as at present understood."[1]

In 1898, after producing a number of films for MaGuire and Baucus, he set up a film-printing laboratory on his own account at Walton-on-Thames. It was in 1899 that he started film production on a very small scale, and H. V. Lawley became his partner about the same time. To begin with, they made for the most part open-air actuality and topical films, 50 ft. in length. By the beginning of the twentieth century the Hepworth Manufacturing Company was turning out roughly one hundred films a year, a quantity which was doubled by 1906.

Hepworth's films increased in length, scope and complexity side by side with those of other producers, but their more thoughtful approach and originality gave him a pre-eminence which increased through the years. Even in these first ten years of British films, he shared with R. W. Paul the honour of being one of the two most important British producers.

Mitchell and Kenyon

The firm of Mitchell and Kenyon, of Lancashire, like Cricks and Sharp (see p. 20), is typical of the small but hardy companies which sprang up early in England and continued to flourish until swamped by the American competition of the early twenties. It was founded in 1897 by James Kenyon and S. Mitchell, and produced all the types of film usual at the time, including a selection of faked topicals of the South African War, filmed on the outskirts of Blackburn.

Some of their films in the later part of this period seem to have been distributed by Charles Urban, and, as in the case of most of the early British companies, a fair number were exported to America. This company,

---

[1] *Animated Photography, or the A.B.C. of the Cinematograph*, 1897, published by Hazell, Watson & Viney, Ltd.

however, has left little trace. On the whole it is probably safe to say that although it made a solid contribution to the considerable British output of the time, it does not seem to have exerted any influence on the development of cinema technique.

Northern Photographic Works, Ltd.

This firm was founded and managed by Birt Acres, whose experimental work with the Kinetic Lantern, and whose early connections with R. W. Paul, fall outside the scope of this work.

Acres does not seem to have been particularly interested in publicising the cinematograph, which he preferred to regard as a scientific invention rather than a music-hall turn. It seems well established, however, that he was very early in the manufacture of both films and cinematograph equipment. The Northern Photographic Works were founded early in 1896. He did not begin to market his cinematographic equipment, however, until the end of 1896, and it was not until 1897 that he was advertising "The Original Animated Photographs." He did not follow up his early successes and little was subsequently heard of him as a maker of films.

Paul's Animatograph Works, Ltd.

R. W. Paul (1869–1943), a scientific instrument maker of Hatton Garden, was one of the first notable British producers. His career in the film world was comparatively short but of extreme importance. Whatever his true place in the story of its technical invention[1] he was indisputably the first Englishman to bring cinematography into the commercial field (see Appendix I). The show given by him at Olympia in March 1896, was the first performance in this country of motion pictures projected on to a screen, at which an admission fee was charged, given by an Englishman. He also seems to have been the first to sell cinematograph apparatus and films.

The output of films from his famous Muswell Hill studio (see p. 30) was not large—some fifty films a year found their way into his main catalogues. These films had world-wide popularity, particularly between 1900 and 1905, the years of his greatest activity. He continued, however,

---

[1] The well-known story of the two Greeks, the kinetoscopes, etc. See B.K.S. lecture of February 3, 1936.

to regard cinematography as a side-line in comparison with his original business of instrument manufacture. The increasing specialization of the film world led to his retirement from it in 1900, and he subsequently achieved distinction in the scientific world.

His importance to the British film industry, which was considerable, was due rather to his business and scientific abilities than to any artistic gifts. Led into film production by force of circumstance, he remained an engineer rather than an artist, and his films seem, from perusal of their detailed synopses, to have been characterized by a lack of either taste or appreciation of the larger possibilities of the cinema, which contrasts strongly with the films of the Hepworth Manufacturing Company. Their worth should not on this account be underrated, however, as they were no doubt well adapted to the level of public appreciation in the cinema's music-hall and fair-ground days.

Sheffield Photo Company

Frank Mottershaw, the owner of a photographic business in Norfolk Street, Sheffield, extended his activities about 1900 to include cinematograph entertainments. Before long he had evolved his own camera and was making some quite successful films. At first he only ventured on simple actuality and topical films, but after a while he bought a tract of land on which he erected a simple stage (see p. 29), and began to write stories for simple made-up films.

Shortly after this Mottershaw's elder son, F. S. Mottershaw, went to London to work with R. W. Paul. Here he gained valuable experience, and a year later returned to Sheffield. He encouraged his father to get larger premises and more modern apparatus. Mr. W. N. Mottershaw writes:

Their first great success was *The Daylight Burglary*, filmed around Sheffield. In one scene the burglar escapes from the hands of his captors by dropping from the foot-bridge of a country railway station on to the roof of a passing train. Mr. Mottershaw became very elated with the result of this film and travelled up to London with the negative. He exhibited it to Mr. Charles Urban, who offered the princely sum of fifty pounds for sale rights, and this was gladly accepted. Such a figure at that time seemed fabulous wealth, and he returned to Sheffield satisfied that his fortune was well in sight.

From then until 1909 the Sheffield Photo Company produced a variety of comedies and adventure films. This isolated, provincial company gained an international reputation, and had agencies all over the world, selling many of its negatives to an American syndicate. It produced some of the most celebrated films of the period, and was one of the first, if not the first, to popularize the chase film.

Walturdaw Company, Ltd.

See under Chapter III. This company did not begin production until July 1905.

Warwick Trading Company

The moving spirit of this company was Charles Urban, an American who originally came to this country to manage the London office of MaGuire and Baucus, the agents for Edison films. About 1898 he re-organized this firm and renamed it the Warwick Trading Company after its offices in Warwick Court, London. His idea was to transform it into an English company, and to this end the Warwick began to make films of its own in England. He dominated it until he broke away to form the Charles Urban Trading Company (see p. 17) early in 1903. While at the Warwick Trading Company, he took over the distribution of Lumière and Star films from France as well as those of James Williamson (see p. 27) and G. A. Smith (see p. 18), both working in Brighton.

Besides acting as agents for films of other makes, while under the enterprising leadership of Urban the Warwick Trading Company was notable for its travel, interest and even advertising films. (The Warwick Blue Book of July 1902, catalogues films advertising Ogden's cigarettes, Bird's custard, Dewar's whiskey and Swan's soap). In the first year of its existence it published some 150 films, including in this number those of Smith and Williamson, but not those of the French makers. By 1903, when Urban left, it was publishing some 500 or 600 films a year, a vastly greater output than that of any other firm, and mainly attributable to its large staff abroad.

For its foreign pictures the W.T.C. had a staff of travelling operators who, taking wars in their stride, became the first war cameramen. The best-known of these was, of course, Joseph Rosenthal. He was not actually the first—in an interview with the writer G. A. Smith specifically stated that John Bennett Stanford (a wealthy amateur) preceded him, sending home the first films of the Boer War, which aroused great enthusiasm when shown at the Alhambra. On the other hand, the 1901 Warwick catalogue refers to Edgar M. Hyman as having sent the "first genuine animated photographs of events in South Africa arriving in England since the war with the Transvaal was declared." Whatever are the true facts of the case, the first film in connection with which Rosenthal is mentioned by name is No. 5545 (i.e. made in April 1900)—which is also the first in the catalogue showing action.[1] The next one, also made by Rosenthal, is equally outstanding in being the first taken behind the Boer lines. From South Africa he hurried to China in time for the Boxer Rebellion, and by Autumn 1900, had taken a series of non-action pictures. By August 1901, the new catalogue contains films from the Philippines, where for some months he had been fraternizing with the U.S. Navy and the natives, with a rapid visit to Australia in May to film the Duke and Duchess of Cornwall arriving at Melbourne.

Others on the foreign staff of the W.T.C. were E. M. Hyman (mentioned above); Sydney Goldman, who replaced Rosenthal in South Africa; F. B. Stewart, operating in India in 1901; John H. Avery, who made a scoop with his film of the Sultan of Morocco in April 1901; Captain Ralph P. Cobbold, who accompanied Emperor Menelik's troops against the "Mad Mullah" in Abyssinia in April 1901; and G. A. Smith and Urban themselves, who toured Italy with a camera early in 1901.

On September 22, 1902, F. Ormiston-Smith led the "Bioscope Expedition" up the Alps. They climbed Mont Blanc and Schreckhorn, and took some remarkable films with a specially-designed camera costing £50. This series received a great deal of publicity as a "perilous adventure in search of Animated Photographs." This reputation seems to have been justified:

... The most remarkable strip of all shows the guides roped together slipping down a precipice. It happened just at the moment the camera was ready for operation, and Mr. Smith, with the greatest sang-froid, continued to turn the handle. "You see," he says, "they were too far off for me to help them. . . ."[2]

---

[1] See p. 66.   [2] *Illustrated Mail*, October 18, 1902.

On January 1, 1906, the Warwick Trading Company was amalgamated with the Autoscope Company, under the managership of Will Barker (see p. 15).

Williamson's Kinematographic Company, Ltd.

James Williamson (1855–1933) had a chemist's shop in Church Road, Hove. Photography was his hobby, and he ran it as a side-line to his main business. Like many others he first took up cinematography in 1896 as a novelty to add to his lantern lectures. In September 1896, he bought a Wrench projector, and in spring of 1897 took a motion picture with the same machine. He apparently did not start selling films until 1898.

In this year he closed down the chemistry side of his business and concentrated on the photographic side, moving to new premises in Western Road, Hove, where he made films in the back yard. A large house called "Ivy Lodge" was rented for a time, and here such films as *Attack on a Chinese Mission Station, Fire!*, and the *Two Naughty Boys* series were made. Williamson himself, with the help of his family, wrote, produced, developed, printed and often acted in his own films. The "two naughty boys" were two of Williamson's own sons.

The retail business in Western Road was sold about 1904, and the Williamsons turned all their attentions to the manufacture of films and apparatus, which was carried on at the Wilbury works (opened in the autumn of 1902). They remained, during the period under review, one of the lesser producing firms, with an approximate total of fifty films a year to their credit.

During this period Williamson films were distributed first by Butcher, then by Gaumont, and later by Urban. It was not until 1907 that they opened their own London office at 27, Cecil Court.

SPECIAL SOURCES OF MATERIAL USED IN CHAPTER I

Autoscope Company.—Interview with W. G. Barker; *Optical Lantern Journal*, December 1905.

Bamforth and Company, Ltd.—*Huddersfield Examiner* (undated).

British Mutoscope and Biograph Company.—Lecture by Colonel Bromhead to the B.K.S. on December 11, 1933.

Charles Urban Trading Company.—Charles Urban Trading Company catalogues; interview with G. A. Smith; G. A. Smith's film list of 1898.

Clarendon Film Company.—B.K.S. lectures; Letter from A. G. Challis.

Esme Collings.—Notebooks of James Williamson; interview with G. A. Smith.

Cricks and Sharp.—Interview with R. H. Cricks; Cricks and Sharp catalogues.

Gaumont and Company.—B.K.S. lectures.

Haggar and Sons.—Lectures to the B.K.S. on December 11, 1933 and February 3, 1936; Gaumont catalogues.

Hepworth Manufacturing Company.—Biographical notes supplied by C. Hepworth; *Animated Photography, the A.B.C. of the Cinematograph*, by C. Hepworth, 1897; Lecture to the B.K.S. by C. Hepworth, February 3, 1936; Hepworth catalogue.

Mitchell and Kenyon.—*Kine Weekly*, March 5, 1925.

Northern Photographic Works, Ltd.—*Photographic News* of January 24, 1896; various photographic journals; letter from Albany Ward; *A.B.C. of the Cinematograph*, by C. Hepworth.

Paul's Animatograph Works, Ltd.—Lecture to the B.K.S. by R. W. Paul on February 3, 1936; *Electronic Engineering*, August 1943; R. W. Paul's catalogues.

Sheffield Photo Company.—Notes supplied by W. N. Mottershaw; letter from P. Longhorn; Sheffield Photo Company's catalogues.

Walturdaw Company, Ltd.—*Optical Lantern Journal*, July 1905.

Warwick Trading Company.—Warwick Trading Company's catalogues; lectures to the B.K.S. of December 11, 1933 and February 3, 1936; interview with W. G. Barker; *Optical Lantern Journal*, December 1905.

Williamson's Kinematographic Company.—Williamson family album, catalogues and notebooks.

CHAPTER TWO

Early Film Studios

Simple actuality and topical films naturally require neither studios, properties nor special lighting, being filmed on the spot. Simple made-up scenes were shot wherever the light was good enough, which in practice meant that they were filmed in the open air. The first made-up film produced for public projection in England, R. W. Paul's *Soldier's Courtship* (see p. 85) was made on the roof of the Alhambra Theatre, and gardens, waste land and actual streets were the setting of many an early film—the picturesque Inn at Ecclesall often appeared in films of the Sheffield Photo Company.

The elaborate studios of later years may be traced back to the small out-door stages which soon began to appear. These were erected by more or less all settled producers around the turn of the century, and facilitated the production of films requiring interior settings. Some idea of the rough-and-ready nature of these early beginnings may best be given by quoting descriptions of three of the most important of them—Hepworth's, the Sheffield Photo Company's and Gaumont's. Cecil Hepworth says of the stage he erected in the garden of his villa in Hurst Grove at Walton-on-Thames in 1898–9:

It consisted of a wooden floor, about 10 ft. by 6 ft., laid down in the tiny back garden with two or three uprights to prop the flats against. The scenery was painted in the kitchen; the smell of the size, incidentally, was a pleasing addition to our food, saving the cost of cheese.[1]

The Sheffield Photo Company stage of about 1900 was of the same type —in a letter to the writer P. Longhorn recalls it as follows:

This consisted of a stage 18 ft. from the ground, about 20 ft. long by 9 ft. wide, the back of the stage was formed by one wall the full length of the stage,

[1] Lecture to the B.K.S., February 3, 1936.

and approximately 14 ft. high, with a further 5 ft. of stage floor behind for on-and-off stage work. This wall was provided with a door and window of the usual household type. This being an open-air studio the wall had to be re-papered for almost every scene taken, and many times when the papering had been finished the light had failed and there was no more work for that day. Owing to this and other difficulties of like nature, interiors were kept out of as many subjects as possible.

This form of studio was fairly general for several years—that of W. G. Barker (see p. 15) was yet another example. It was a short step from this to the glass studio—"a veritable Crystal Palace," as someone was sure to call it—developed by several of the more important producers in the opening years of the twentieth century. It seems possible that the first in the country was that of the Mutoscope and Biograph Company behind the old Tivoli by the Adelphi Arches. According to F. W. Baker:

Studio built about 1897 at the back of the old Tivoli, Strand, for the American Biograph Company:—The studio revolved on the cup and ball principle (an old stage device). The ball being bolted to a cement bed, the cup fixed to the centre of the floor and well black-leaded, at each corner was a detachable wheel which ran on a flat circular plate flush with the ground. This enabled the Studio to turn in any direction for the best light. The glass part of the Studio was put together in sections, easily taken apart, the idea being to stage any out-door set such as part of a ship, etc., by detaching the wheels, the cup and ball device enabled the floor to be moved up or down or in any direction, giving a perfect movement of a ship at sea.[1]

This studio was apparently unique. The more usual type was a stage of roughly 28 by 15 feet, with glass roof or walls to admit the maximum amount of sunlight, and sliding doors which could be opened on a fine day. Both J. Williamson (see p. 27) and G. A. Smith (see p. 18), working at Brighton—the former at Wilbury Road and the latter at St. Anne's Well Gardens—had studios of this type with rails at the front on which the stage could be extended in the manner of an apron-stage.

R. W. Paul's famous studio at Sydney Road, New Southgate, built in 1899[2] was one of the first of this type. It had a glass roof and sliding doors, but was equipped for trick effects, with consequent structural differences:

[1] Letter to the writer.   [2] R. W. Paul's lecture to the B.K.S., February 3, 1936.

It comprised a miniature stage, about 28 ft. by 14 ft., raised above the ground level and protected by an iron building with wide sliding doors and a glass roof facing north. At the rear of the stage was a hanging frame on which back cloths, pained in monochrome, could be fixed; the frame could be lowered through a slot to facilitate the work of the scene painter. Traps in the stage, and a hanging bridge above it, provided means for working certain effects to which I will refer later. Eventually a scene-painting room was added behind the studio. A trolley mounted on rails carried the camera, which could thus be set at any required distance from the stage, to suit the subject. Sometimes the trolley was run to or from the stage while the picture was being taken, thus giving a gradual enlargement or reduction of the image on the film.[1]

This reference to a mobile camera is of particular interest. As late as 1912 or 1913 anything but a perfectly static camera was frowned upon: but it seems from this remark of Paul's and certain other indications, that a mobile camera was not entirely unthought of even in the very early period.

Incidentally, it was quite usual in those days for the producer to hire his studio out by the day to private persons, and R. W. Paul's 1902 catalogue contains the following announcement:

The large studio, adjoining my new Southgate works, is at the disposal of customers requiring the production of special advertising or other scenes, and is provided with paint rooms for full-sized scenery, under the supervision of a competent artist, and a stock of about fifty backgrounds ready for use. The stage-traps, bridges and wings enable any stage performance to be animato-graphed, as will be seen by the description of many of my new subjects below, all of which were produced here. This building, erected to my own designs, which is the only one of the kind in this country, enables the photographic effects to be perfectly controlled.

Towards 1903–4 the possibilities of powerful artificial lighting were being realized and the indoor studio was making its appearance, though still in a very rudimentary form. The Mutoscope and Biograph Company moved from the studio described above to an indoor studio at 107, Regent Street, and Hepworth also had an indoor studio which may, indeed, have been the first in the country:

[1] R. W. Paul's lecture to the B.K.S., February 3, 1936.

The first covered studio at Walton was one of the first anywhere, the honour being shared by Paul of England and the Vitagraph Company of America. Anyhow the date was about 1903, and I will leave it at that . . . the studio (was) on the first floor. It was glazed with muranese glass to diffuse the sunlight and cast no shadows. It had auxiliary lighting from ten open-type arc lamps.[1]

[1] C. Hepworth's lecture to the B.K.S., February 3, 1936.

1. Portraits

R. W. PAUL

CECIL HEPWORTH

G. A. SMITH

CHARLES URBAN

2. Portraits

WALTER HAGGAR

E. G. TURNER

G. H. CRICKS

J. ROSENTHAL

. Williamson's studio with
floor partly drawn out into
the open

The same studio closed—

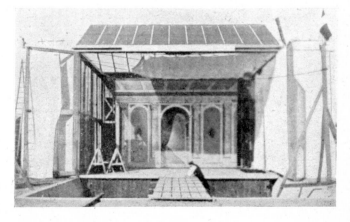

or with the floor wholly
under glass (1902)

4. Film Production in Brighton

G. A. Smith's
studio

Set for
Mary Jane's Mishap

Scene in
Mary Jane's Mishap
where sweep's brush
comes through
chimney

G. A. Smith arrang-
ng a "set scene,"
1901

Set for *Dorothy's
Dream*, G. A. SMITH

Still from *Dorothy's
Dream*, G. A. SMITH

6. Film Studios

R. W. Paul's Studio, 1902

J. Williamson's Studio, 1902

7. Exhibition

The Mottershaw family setting out to give an animatograph display

A travelling film show

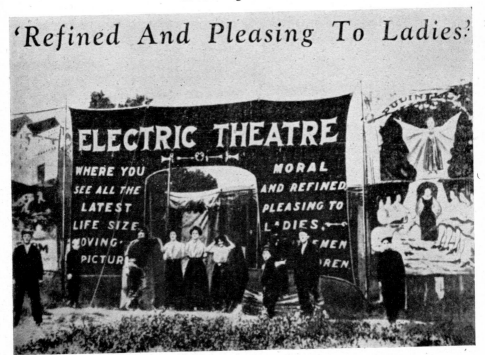

8. Exhibition

Walter Haggar's fairground show in 1902—

and in 1906

9. Programmes of 1896

ASSEMBLY ROOMS, CHELTENHAM.

PROGRAMME

Cheltenham Cricket Club

CONCERT

AND

LIST OF PICTURES OF

PAUL'S THEATROGRAPH
(Animated Photographs).

TUESDAY, DECEMBER 1st, 1896, at Eight o'clock.

Patrons:

THE MAYOR (Colonel Rogers).

TICKETS 2/6 (Reserved), 1/-, Back Seats 6d.

Tickets may be obtained and Plan of Room may be seen at Woodward's Music Warehouse, Promenade, Cheltenham.

NEXT WEEK ! !

AT

THE EMPIRE.

Once Again at Great Expense,

THE ORIGINAL . .

. . UNSURPASSED . .

. . UNEQUALLED

. LUMIERE .

CINEMATOGRAPHE

From the Empire, London,

Under the Direction of M. TREWEY.

A Series of Brilliant and Interesting Scenes absolutely true to life in
PRECISION, PROPORTION AND MOTION.

Towerskay in Moscow.	Soldiers' Parade in Madrid.
Children—Cat and Dog.	Concorde Bridge, Paris.
The Disappointed Artist.	Lancers in Stuttgart.
Burmese Dance at the Crystal Palace.	Artillery in Barcelona.
	Fire Brigade Call, London.
Hamburg Bridge, Germany.	Charge of Cavalry in France.

AND

. A Remarkable Picture—" TOBOGGANING IN SWITZERLAND."

You would have to expend a large amount of money and time to obtain a
view of the Scenes of the above Programme in their Geographical situation, but
by the aid of this wonderful instrument in conjunction with Motor Photography,
they are brought before you exact in form and motion for the money and time a
visit to the Empire entails.

Tudor Printing Works, Cardiff. 14910

Cheltenham's Latest Improvements!

Acknowledged by both the General Public and all the Press, to be THE

Grandest Forward Stroke of the Day

❖❖❖❖❖❖❖❖❖❖❖❖❖❖❖❖❖❖❖❖❖❖❖❖

COME TO THE
ASSEMBLY ROOMS,
☞ *AFTERNOON or EVENING!*

❖❖❖❖❖❖❖❖❖❖❖❖❖❖❖❖❖❖❖❖❖❖❖❖

You can	**MEET THE PARIS EXPRESS, at Calais,**
To see	**THE FIRE BRIGADE, called out.**
Then back to	**WESTMINSTER, take the first 'Bus**
For	**PRINCESS MAUD'S WEDDING, after that**
To	**HAMPSTEAD HEATH, in time**
To see	**TOMMY ADKINS' COURTSHIP, Then with**
The crowd to	**THE DERBY—A Grand Race!!**
The	**GORDON HIGHLANDERS, pass you on the way**
To the	**MUSIC HALL SPORTS, and many Other events.**

We are Changing our Programme.

SHOWING NEW PICTURES! ☜
☞ ENGAGING THE BEST ARTISTES!
And Giving a FISRT-RATE ENTERTAINMENT!

The Cheltenham Cricket Club ask your support.

THURSDAY, FRIDAY & SATURDAY—Afternoon & Evening.

COURT THEATRE,

[see and Manageress] **NEW ROAD, BRIGHTON.** [MRS. M. BARRASFORD.

ENORMOUS SUCCESS.   THE TALK OF BRIGHTON.

The World in Motion

THE RAGE OF PARIS.

TIMES & PRICES:	**EVER ADVANCING!!**
COMMENCING	**Always Up-to-Date.**
Monday, March 2,	SUPERB SCENERY. BRILLIANT MUSIC.
And **DAILY** at	NEW ILLUMINATED SONGS.

☞ **3**

Doors open at 2.30,

A Tour through North Wales

☞ **7**

Doors open at 6.30,

TULIPS

A BEAUTIFULLY COLOURED PICTURE.

☞ **9**

Doors open at 8.45.

The Cabman's Delusions

I wonder how it is done.

Admission Prices:

1/6 1/= 6d. 3d.

Children Half-Price to all parts,
Gallery excepted.
No seats guaranteed unless booked.
No Money returned.

THE AUXETO

The LATEST VOICE PRODUCING MACHINE.

FROM EARTH to MOON

The Latest Fantastic Picture.

THE CABIN BOY

A TALE OF THE SEA.

✳ WORK MADE EASY ✳

The Last Cartridge

A Story of the Indian Mutiny, depicting the bravery shown by
a handful of Troops, who held the Fort until the last men and women, rather than
fall into the enemy's hands, were about to take their own lives, but **The Gallant
Highlanders** came at the nick of time and saved the fall of the Fort.

The **CHAMPION TENOR,** A Man with a Very Strong Voice.

FATHERHOOD

A Drama in Pictures.

SUPPLEMENTED BY ADVANCED VAUDEVILLE ARTISTES.

CONSTANT CHANGE of PROGRAMME

COME EARLY TO SECURE A GOOD SEAT

☞ OUR MOTTO: TO INTEREST AND TO AMUSE.

Smoking allowed in all parts.   **No Early Doors.**

The Management reserve the right to refuse admission.   Box Office open daily from 10 a.m.
Nat. Tel. 366,

Stage Manager and Electrician		For THE			Mr. D. Dwain
Operator	}	WORLD	{	... ...	Mr. Adams
Bill Inspector ...		IN		... ...	Mr. Wheeler
ACTING MANAGER ...	}	MOTION.	{	... ...	MR. A. ROSENTHAL

Emery & Son, Ltd., "Gazette" Office, Hove.

To-Night! To-Night!

CALDER'S FAMOUS

CINEMATOGRAPH

AND

Popular Concert.

Don't miss seeing the Grand NEW PICTURES of

THE DREYFUS COURT MARTIAL.

The Prince of Wales in Edinburgh.
Sir Redvers Buller Embarking for Transvaal.
Scenes at the Highland Brigade Camp.
The Invercharron Gathering.
The Grand Fire Dance.
Barnum & Bailey's Procession.
The Mysterious Astrologer's Dream.
Spendid Train Scenes.
Grand Coloured Dances.
Comicalities and Burlesque Scenes, &c., &c.

Pictures of absorbing interest and Astounding Transformations.

SPLENDID • CONCERT
By First-Class Artistes.

DOORS OPEN AT 7.30.   CONCERT AT 8 P.M.
Popular Prices See Bills.

A BRIGHT UP-TO-DATE SPARKLING ENTERTAINMENT

14. Posters of 1898 and 1900

ALHAMBRA THEATRE
STOURBRIDGE. Mr PATCH

MONDAY, FEBRUARY 7th, 1898
SIX NIGHTS ONLY. ENORMOUS ATTRACTIONS. VISIT OF

D'ARCY'S
— GRAND —

DIORAMA

INCLUDING
PORTSMOUTH HARBOUR | THE 'NANSEN' EXPEDITION
MATABELE WAR | Sunrise in the Bay of Biscay
OUR INDIAN EMPIRE | MALTA
The Nautch Dance | DELHI, THE ROME OF ASIA
Constantinople, the City of Mosques. | The Great Imbara' Palace
| LUCKNOW, etc., etc.

— MUSICAL —

D'ARCYS

ARLENO

ANNIE BELL

PROF. DENT

CINEMATOGRAPH

MONS. BERT | Mr. B. Sivol

MADAME VALDA

THE
EXCELSIOR COMBINATION
IN A SCREAMING SKETCH

TIME AND PRICES AS USUAL

INFANT
SCHOOLROOM
MICKLEOVER. 1900

One Night Only, WEDNESDAY, Feb. 7th. at 8.
Doors open at 7.30.

Great Attraction!

THE EXCELSIOR
DIORAMAS
And Great American
BIOSCOPE

The above Exhibition is a Good First-class Entertainment, and
free from Vulgarity throughout.

The First Part consists of

TOUR ROUND THE WORLD!

Consisting of over
100 Scenes 100
Beautifully shown by Limelight. Splendid Effects!

Sights of London. Paris. Rome. Constantinople, Beautiful Sights of
VENICE.

A Visit to the HOLY LAND

Scenes of Joppa, or Jaffa, which is the principal Seaport of Palestine, and landing
place for most Visitors to the Holy Land. Views of Jerusalem, Mount of Olives,
Mosque of Omar, and the Holy Sepulchre, Bethlehem, Nazareth, &c.

Cairo & the Pyramids, a Splendid journey through the Suez Canal
en route to India. Malta, Jenoa Gibraltar and the beautiful Island
of Maderia.

A delightful journey through Hong Kong, Singapore, Pekin, Joko-
hama, New Zealand, Sydney, Melbourne, San Francisco, the
Josemite Valley, and States of California.

Also a visit to the Salt Lake City, and other principal places of
Interest of the World.

Concluding with a Series of Living Pictures on the great American

BIOSCOPE

War Scenes, Comic Scenes, Interesting Scenes of all sorts, with all
the latest and up-to-date Pictures added

Refined, High-class & Thrilling Entertainment !

Admission, Front Seats 1/- Second 6d., Back 3d.

CHILDREN'S PERFORMANCE
At 5.30.
Admission 1d. Adults 3d.

Proprietor   Mr. WALTER FEARN.

ROYAL DRILL HALL, DERBY.

Mr. WALLER JEFFS' NEW CENTURY

PICTURES

FINEST ANIMATED EXHIBITION IN THE WORLD.

ATTENTION!
SHORT SEASON ONLY!

TIMES & PRICES:
Commencing
MONDAY, JAN. 13
And until further notice.
EVERY NIGHT
At 8 o'clock.
Early Doors open at 7.
Ordinary Doors at 7-30.

MATINEES:
Saturdays at 3.
Doors open 2-30.

ADMISSION PRICES:
2/- 1/6 1/- 6d.
CHILDREN HALF PRICE.
Promenade (Limited) 3d.

RESERVED SEATS Booked at EDGAR
HORNE's MUSIC WAREHOUSE, The Strand,
Derby.

No Seats Guaranteed unless Booked.
No Money Returned.

EVER ADVANCING ! ! !
ALWAYS UP-TO-DATE.

SUPERB SCENERY !
BRILLIANT MUSIC ! !
NEW ILLUMINATED SONGS ! ! !

The TWO ORPHANS

The Beauties of
BONNIE **SCOTLAND**

Expensive Engagement of
Miss L. CASEY
Soprano Vocalist.

Mr. GEO. MARTINI - Pianist

Mr. WALTER
ROSELLE
Lecturer and Humorist.

Mr. F. FIELD - Baritone Vocalist
LATEST COMIC PICTURES.
GORGEOUS PANTOMIME.

Wreck of H.M.S. 'MONTAGU.'

Just added, at enormous expense, the **World's Greatest Glove Contest:**

Tommy BURNS v. Gunner MOIR
The most Exciting and Interesting Picture of its class ever taken.

☞ CONSTANT CHANGE OF PROGRAMME.

NORTH AMERICA and its Natural Wonders.
VOYAGE ACROSS the ATLANTIC. GEYSERS of the YELLOWSTONE
☞ THE ENCHANTED GLASSES. LITTLE DORA. ☜

The POLICE DOGS OF PARIS

| 100,000 | ANIMATED PHOTOGRAPHS PERFECTLY PROJECTED. | 100,000 |

BRILLIANT ELECTRIC ILLUMINATIONS. SPARKLING MUSIC.

The pick of the PICTURE WORLD. EVERYONE Amazed and Delighted
The Press unanimous in its Praise. All former Productions Surpassed.

COME EARLY TO SECURE A GOOD SEAT.
OUR MOTTO! To INTEREST and to AMUSE ! ! !

Electrician and Operator	For Mr.	... Mr. W. ROSENTHAL.
Advance Agent	WALLER JEFFS' NEW	... Mr. W. DAWES.
Musical Director	CENTURY PICTURES.	... Mr. GEO. MARTINI.
Stage Manager	(Title Registered and	... Mr. MARTIN.
ACTING MANAGER	Copyright).	... Mr. H. S. CHAMBERS.

Malawaring & Valentine Ltd., John Bright Street, Birmingham.

16. Actuality and Interest Films

Exploding a Submarine Mine. R. W. PAUL 1901–2

Emigrants on an Upper Deck. C.U.T.C., 1905

The Wild Men of Borneo. C.U.T.C., 1903

CHAPTER THREE

Market Conditions

The modern structure of the film industry—producer, distributor, and exhibitor, with distributor renting films to the exhibitor for a given period of showing—took a good deal longer than the first ten years to develop, and throughout this period free sale by producer ("manufacturer") to showman was the prevailing custom. Certainly, both film hire and "exclusive" rights in one form or another appeared early in the period. But by 1906 it was still the general rule for film makers to issue their own catalogues, print any number of copies of each film, and sell them outright to the travelling showmen, music-hall exhibitors or anyone else who cared to place an order. From the beginning a good deal of foreign trade was carried on, and some of Paul's catalogues even contained announcements in German. Films were sold at so much a foot, usually 6d. or 8d. for the export trade. Reductions were made as the film aged, as all films, even topicals, remained in circulation for a considerable time. A topical selling at 6d. a foot in 1903 might be 3d. a foot or even less three years later.

The origin of film rental is to be found in the accumulation by exhibitors of superfluous stocks of old films, which they used for secondary shows or hiring out to other showmen. The process can be illustrated by the development of the first renting company in this country, "Walturdaw."

J. D. Walker and E. G. Turner were exploiting the Edison kinetoscope and phonograph early in 1896. In July they turned their attention to the new craze of cinematography, and bought Wrench's first projector. They toured the country as the North American Entertainment Company, giving cinema shows in towns and villages, using first Edison subjects, and later mainly Lumière films. At first they aimed at the better-class audiences, but business was bad and in January 1897, they reformed as "Walker and Turner," with a new policy of playing to the gallery instead of to the stalls. This was so successful that by the end of 1897 they were doing well and had three machines. It was about this time that they began to rent films out to their fellow showmen. E. G. Turner's own account of this is as follows:

The price of films quickly dropped from 1s. to 8d. per foot, and then became standard at 6d. per foot; this allowed us to increase our store, but it soon became evident that to have to provide new films every time we took a repeat engagement was too expensive. So we conceived the idea, first of all, of an interchange with other exhibitors, who experienced the same difficulty in regard to new supplies. From this we eventually evolved the renting of films to other people, because we found that we had by far a larger stock than any of the other men. By buying films regularly we could use them ourselves and hire them to the other people, and so in such small beginnings was evolved the great renting system as known to-day. . . . We would buy as many as ten and twelve prints of an interesting subject, and on one occasion we actually bought eighty prints of a film, which was entitled *Landing an Old Lady from a Small Boat*. . . We then extended operations to the entertainment bureaus, such as Whiteley's, Keith Prowse, Harrods, Gamage, Webster and Girling, H. L. Toms, Woods of Cheapside, Ashton and Mitchell, Army and Navy Stores, the Church Mission Halls, Salvation Army, the Leysian Mission, City Road, and many more. . . .[1]

By 1898 they were hiring out "sets"—previously selected programmes lasting anything from two minutes to half an hour, of films from all makers, and of all types. £2 10s. per 1,000 feet per night was the rate finally fixed.[2]

The experience of other exhibitors was similar, and the most famous of early renters, Jury's Imperial Pictures, began in exactly the same way although a few years later, in 1905–6. Walker and Turner began the hire of films in 1897, and in the same year Cecil Hepworth's *A.B.C of Cinematography* contained an advertisement for "Films on Hire" from Noakes and Norman of Greenwich. Film hire, in other words, is almost as old as films themselves. Even so, the distributing side of the industry even at the end of the period under review bears little resemblance to its modern structure. The impulse towards film hire came from the exhibiting side, and it was exhibitors who became renters. They had no power to stop the free sale of films by the producers, in fact their own stocks were built up in the open market. Thus it came about that identical films were both for sale and for hire at the same time. The conception of exclusive rights entered the industry as exclusive selling rather than exclusive renting

---

[1] *Kine Weekly*, June 17, 1926.
[2] Walturdaw became film producers in July 1905. See p. 25.

rights. Frequently a producer, besides selling his own films directly, used some large film company as a selling agent (e.g. James Williamson and the Charles Urban Trading Company), or even sold through several agents at the same time. In late 1904 Gaumont's secured the exclusive selling rights of all Mutoscope and Biograph Company films, including the product of the American and German branches of this company. The modern system of exclusive renting rights, however, was still many years ahead.

CHAPTER FOUR

Showmanship

Throughout this period, places of exhibition fell into several main categories—fair-grounds, music-halls and other local halls, and disused shops. The music-hall was the commercial cinema's first home. The first paid show itself, the Lumière Cinematograph shown by Trewey at the Polytechnic on February 20, 1896, was transferred on March 9th to the Empire, Leicester Square, where it ran for eighteen months. At the same time Paul's machine ran for two years at the Alhambra, where it had started on March 25, 1896.

Film shows were for a time included in the programmes of other music-halls throughout the country, usually as one item of twenty to thirty minutes towards the end of the performance. A. D. Thomas of the Royal Canadian Biograph Company, William Jury, Walter Gibbons at the Moss Empires and the London Hippodrome, Payne, Matt Raymond and Ruffells exhibited films in this way, and the British Mutoscope and Biograph Company ran a turn for years at the Palace Theatre, London. In the latter part of the period £3 was a fair average price for one turn. It was quite a frequent practice for an operator to give several turns a night, rushing his projector and films by cab from theatre to theatre.

Some of this class of showmen went far afield—A. D. Thomas took a show to the West Indies and Canada, and T. J. West of the Modern Marvel Company travelled in Australasia. There was a good deal of overlapping between this and the third category mentioned above—that of showmen travelling from town to town, hiring local halls for their shows and staying as long as the audiences lasted. Many of these shows, having found a good market, became more or less permanent. Names remembered in this connection are those of Maskelyne, at Egyptian Hall; Alfred J. West's "Our Navy" at the Polytechnic; Ralph Pringle with the Biograph Company; Sidney Carter; Waller Jeffs with the New Century Pictures; George Black; and Arthur Cunningham. Other showmen gave perfor-

mances at private parties—David Devant's price for this type of show was
£25 an evening.

Programmes were elementary, and to some extent it is certainly true to
say that the mere movement of the pictures was sufficiently enthralling
to the unsophisticated audiences of the time. Press notices tell how easily
they were amused, for hours on end:

So animated and real that one sat spell-bound.

The views were very clear and the action represented was so realistic that in
several cases the audience could scarce restrain their wonder, and even startled
surprise at the events which were flashed before their eyes.

A succession of scenes representing recent historical events, panoramic views
of objects and places of note, with beautiful dissolving views of floral groups,
etc., kept the audience interested and amused for over two hours.[1]

Even so, many showmen found that after the first few months public
interest faded slightly and it was necessary to engage musicians and music-
hall artists to fill the programme out—Jury's practice is one example of
this, and even the programme[2] described above so enthusiastically was
liberally interspersed with "humorous songs" and "musical speciality
acts."

There was a time when the popularity of the cinematograph as a music-
hall and village concert turn was on the wane. It seemed as if, now that
the novelty was wearing off, films were good only for "chasers" to be
turned on as the audience was filing out. It is to the fairground showmen
that the cinema owes its ultimate success. The new toy, a passing fancy in
the music-halls, became a firmly established feature of the fairgrounds.
It was they who bridged the gap between the music hall days and the later,
more respectable picture palaces, and they disappeared only with the
First World War—long after the coming of the regular cinema.

Randall Williams[3] was probably the first to exhibit cinematograph films
under canvas. It was soon taken up by many others, and the fair-day
crowds, already accustomed to ghost shows and marionettes, now packed
into the tent, standing or sitting on the grass, to gaze at the screen hanging
from the king-pole. At the peak of their popularity, there were six separate
cinema shows at Nottingham Goose Fair alone. The showmen who worked

---

[1] Local Scottish newspapers.
[2] Robert Calder's.   [3] See p. 118.

the fairgrounds were known throughout the country—William Taylor, John Proctor, George Green, George Kemp, Sophie Hancock, and many others. Some such as Pat Collins, Harry J. Scard, and Richard Dooner, later founded cinema circuits. Walter Haggar, the famous showman of South Wales, became well-known as a producer as well as an exhibitor (see p. 21). Many of these men acquired considerable wealth, and travelled with equipment worth tens of thousands of pounds. Some even had their own organs, electricity dynamos, and elaborate pavilions with gilded fronts, sloping floors, plush drapings and seats for anything up to four or five hundred people. The projectors were worked hard from early morning until late at night, and yet the enterprise and skill of these travelling exhibitors was such that towards the end of the period under review the average show was technically first-class.

The fair-ground showmen were a picturesque, rough-and-ready lot. According to Colonel Bromhead:

Sometimes it was difficult to collect accounts from them. A representative meeting a showman who was behind with his account was immediately invited to "come and collect it yourself." That representative spent a couple of days on the round-abouts collecting the amount due, in tuppences. It was not at all unusual to wait all day until the money for the film just sold had been collected and to stay in the pay-box or round the show while it was coming in.[1]

From 1904, when Colonel Bromhead's theatre was built in Bishopsgate Street, special theatres for films and nothing else began to appear, called variously "electric palaces," "bioscope theatres," and so on. The dramatic describers of the travelling shows, the piano accompaniment, the plush seats and the darkened hall began to cater for a special film audience, apart from the fair-ground crowds and music-hall patrons. For some years yet, however, they were to continue side-by-side with the fairs, the music-halls and that other home of the cinema, the unused shop. George Pearson describes his first visit to "the pictures" as follows:

It was outside a derelict greengrocer's shop. The hawk-eyed gentleman on a fruit crate was bewildering a sceptical crowd. In that shuttered shop there was a miracle to be seen for a penny, but only twenty-four could enter at a time;

[1] Lecture to the B.K.S., December 11, 1933.

there wasn't room for more. His peroration was magnificent; "You've seen pictures of people in books, all frozen stiff. You've never seen people come alive in pictures, moving about natural like you and me. Well, go inside and see for yourself living pictures for a penny. Then tell me if I'm a liar."

One of my pennies went suddenly: I joined twenty-three other sceptics inside. Stale cabbage leaves and the smell of dry mud gave atmosphere to a scene for Hogarth. A furtive youth did things to a tin oven on iron legs, and a white sheet swung from the ceiling. We grouped around the oven and wondered. Suddenly things happened; someone turned down a gas jet, and the tin apparatus burst into a fearful clatter, and an oblong picture slapped on to the sheet and began a violent dance. After a while you discerned it was a picture of a house, but a house on fire. Flames and smoke belched from the windows, and someone mounted a fire escape, little human figures darted about below, and the . . . bang! Everything ended. The light went up. The show was over. Exactly one minute. I had been to the cinema![1]

[1] *Sight and Sound*, Winter 1938.

PART TWO

THE FILMS THEMSELVES

CHAPTER ONE

Introduction

When people first went to the pictures, they went to see a novelty. But they stayed for other reasons—curiosity about the world they could not see, the desire for information, or the age-old desire to be told a story. The new story-telling medium involved the gradual emergence of a new technique and the perfection of this, whether explicitly recognized or not, meant in fact the existence of a new art. At first the power of the film-maker over his audience's attention and emotions, by his infinite choice of shots and the way he joined them together, was completely unrealized. Even in a made-up subject the film was seen merely as a combination of the still camera and the stage, and the social and occupational backgrounds of the majority of film makers—portrait photographers, chemists, engineers, lantern lecturers—was not such as to make artistic exploration likely.

In the history of the film one has a unique opportunity to trace the steps by which the elementary technique of a new art forces itself upon its unprepared exponents. The film manufacturers, as they stumbled inevitably on the devices proper to the telling of a story or an idea by means of a celluloid film, almost all misunderstood and misused their discoveries, and exploited as tricks and theatrical effects what should in fact have been integral elements of a new medium. Cecil Hepworth, almost alone, may be excepted from this, for although rarely first in the field, when he did finally adopt new effects he did so with a more truly cinematic approach than the others. It is worth noting that R. W. Paul, usually acclaimed as the greatest British film pioneer, is shown by the content of his films to have had a complete lack of perception in this respect.

Before quoting examples of the different types of early British film as described in the synopses of the producers' catalogues, it is important to realize that the enormous number of films produced (several thousands were made in this country between 1896 and 1906) represents largely the repetition of certain conventional types of subject which had proved successful, and of treatments which emphasized simple demonstrations of movement or satisfied simple curiosity about persons, places and events. Many of the main types of early film were represented in the original Lumière programme shown by Trewey at the Polytechnic on February 20, 1896. For example:

Actuality: *Workers leaving the Lumière Factory, and other items*
Topical: *Congress of Photographic Societies.*
Comedy: *Watering the Gardener.*

Interest films were, if anything, a slightly later development. The distinction between an early actuality, a topical and an interest film soon becomes defined. An actuality results from placing the camera in front of objects which provide movement, a street scene, a train, a boat. The interest arises merely from the curiosity of seeing familiar sights reproduced on the screen: Lumière's train arriving at the station, his boat tossing on the sea, or the crowd emerging from his factory (was this the first advertising film as well!) have no further interest to his contemporary audiences than this. A topical film, on the other hand, covers an event which has news value: when Lumière filmed the Congress of Photographic Societies and Paul the Derby of 1896 the interest was in something wider than mere movement. Undoubtedly the popularity of films with the public rapidly outstripped mere casual curiosity in familiar sights, and developed as events which aroused public interest and which only a few could attend, appeared in living motion on the screen. An interest film, on the other hand, is the earliest form of a documentary treatment: it is the beginning of a film-study of a subject, implying elementary selection and presentation of the living scene. It could emerge equally well from a more careful treatment of a news event or a more selective treatment of actuality. It implies a measure of interpretation, however simple. Examples are Williamson's *Country Life Series* (1899)[1] or even R. W. Paul's *Cory* (1898)[2] where attention is drawn to the subject of the picture rather than to the picture itself.

 Trick films were also a slightly later development. G. A. Smith's use of double exposure by September 1898[3] in a group of films (*Cinderella and*

---

[1] See p. 55.   [2] See p. 54.   [3] Date determined by early cash book.

the Fairy Godmother, The Mesmerist, The Corsican Brothers, etc.)[1] seems
to have been the first effort in this direction, and J. Williamson had made
an isolated trick film by September 1899 (*The Clown Barber*)[2]. But Paul,
who was probably the chief British exponent of the trick film, was comparatively late in starting and was preceded by the French producer
Méliès. Paul's first group (*The Haunted Curiosity Shop,* etc.) appears
to have been made in 1899 or early 1900. Hepworth, also, does not seem
to have first used trick effects until early 1900 (*The Conjuror and the
Boer*). Trick films, usually playing for humour, were in fact the beginnings
of a more elastic use of the camera, once the potentialities of the medium
for sleight-of-eye, sleight-of-action and sleight-of-timing were realized.

Thus apart from the interest film (a development of either the actuality
or the topical film) and the trick film (a development of camera technique),
all main types of film were present from the earliest days, and have pro-
gressed side by side throughout their history.

The length of the films, of course, was a matter of some importance, as
indicated in the producers' catalogues:

Paul	Catalogue of 1898	Average length about 40 to 80 ft. (running time $\frac{2}{3}$ to $1\frac{1}{4}$ minutes approx.).
	Catalogue of 1902	Average length about 100 ft. (running time $1\frac{2}{3}$ minutes).
	Catalogue of 1906	Length up to 650 ft. (running time 11 minutes approx.).
Williamson	Catalogue of 1899	Average length about 60 to 75 ft. (running time 1 to $1\frac{1}{4}$ minutes).
	Catalogue of 1902	Length up to 280 feet (running time $4\frac{1}{2}$ minutes approx.).

Hepworth commenced with fifty-foot films (running time $\frac{5}{6}$ min.), but
by 1906 was making films of up to 850 feet (running time $14\frac{1}{6}$ mins.).

In general, it was not until 1903–4 that films of 400 or 500 feet were
produced, and even then they were fairly exceptional. To make a film of
this length was ambitious, and such films received a good deal of extra
publicity. They were all dramatic, or dramatic-documentary in type.
Probably the longest films of the period prior to 1906 were the Hepworth

[1] See p. 78.   [2] See p. 79.

Company's *Falsely Accused*[1] made between February and June, 1905 (850 feet), and the two versions of *The Life of Charles Peace*[2] made in 1905.

It is, of course, only possible to make tentative assertions about dates and personalities in the development of film technique at this period. It is important to realize that most of the films themselves have long since disintegrated or been destroyed or lost,[3] and that conclusions have to be based mainly on the few surviving films and the film catalogues of the time. This, however, yields better results than would at first appear possible. Producers were in the habit of giving an elaborate synopsis of every film in their catalogues, and in the days when even a 50-foot film was given its descriptive paragraph or so, it may reasonably be assumed that any features of importance will have been mentioned. For example, when a close-up was almost unheard of, you may be sure the daring producer who took a "head-and-shoulders portrait" would draw the prospective buyers' attention to the fact. It will in fact be seen (Chapter II) that the synopses, which are quoted in full, are remarkably complete.

A further difficulty is that the films are not dated, which has made it difficult to determine the relative stages of development of the various producers. But because they are almost always numbered or arranged in the catalogues chronologically, it has been possible, by ascertaining the dates of those dealing with news events, to date the other films within limits of varying range. Thus the analysis in this and the following chapter may safely be considered reliable, but any conclusions about the "first" close-up, the "first" trick film, and so on must be treated cautiously as the collection of catalogues used,[4] although comprehensive, is of course not complete, and in any case the producers did not always include every film in their general lists.

Bearing this in mind, it is interesting to see how much earlier many developments appeared than is commonly supposed. As already stated, the germs of all types of film were present from the beginning, and the "made-up film" or rehearsed scene (see p. 85) was as early as the actuality or topical, though not so frequent until the turn of the century. R. W.

---

[1] See p. 100. [2] See p. 105.
[3] See Appendix V for examples of films preserved by the N.F.L.
[4] See Appendix V for catalogues used, and method used to date films.

Paul's *Soldier's Courtship*,[1] a comic scene, was made in March 1896, and the first film in J. Williamson's catalogue (i.e. 1897) is *Two Naughty Boys Upsetting the Spoons*. C. Hepworth, on the other hand, did not produce a made-up scene until No. 72 in his catalogue, *The Stolen Drink* (before the end of 1899).[2]

In this connection it is interesting to note the preference of British producers for films taken out-of-doors, and the influence this had on the appearance and popularity of the chase or rescue film. The earliest made-up films, like topicals and actualities, were almost all out-door scenes. It was towards the end of the century that the little open-air stages which made indoor sets possible were coming into fashion. Strangely enough, the earliest use of indoor settings seems to have been for filmed vaudeville turns. On the whole, however, British producers were inclined to turn to the country lanes, the race-tracks, gipsy camps, the fair on Hampstead Heath, and the streets for their drama. This favoured producers like Walter Haggar (see p. 21), who moved from place to place and had no permanent studio. It has been suggested that the tradition of the open-air was not without significance in the development of the chase film. The earliest film of this well-known pattern that it has been possible to trace is J. Williamson's *Fire* [3] (January 1902). C. Hepworth made a similar film towards the end of 1903—*Firemen to the Rescue*—and, of course, his famous *Rescued by Rover*[4] is itself a chase film. Between September and November of 1903 the Sheffield Photo Company started a long and successful series of chase films with *Daring Daylight Burglary*.[5] Gaumont also produced a large number of good examples, including one in July or August 1903 (*The Runaway Match, or Marriage by Motor*, produced by Alfred Collins), which is of special interest in that the chase is shown in two "sections"—the first taken from the car of the pursued, and the second from that of the pursuers. W. Haggar and G. H. Cricks were other producers who made outstanding examples of this type of film, from the latter part of 1903 onwards. It is interesting that R. W. Paul, who was more interested in the use of the technical possibilities of the cinema for magical than for dramatic effect, seems to have produced only a few belated examples of the chase (*A Victim of Misfortune*, December 1905).

[1] See p. 85. [2] See p. 92. [3] See p. 98. [4] See p. 109. [5] See p. 103.

The introduction of separate scenes as part of a single narrative, essential to chase and rescue films, had taken several years to mature. The earliest made-up films consisted of only one scene, and a change of scene did not appear until about 1901 (C. Hepworth, J. Williamson) although Paul produced a film in 1898–9 (*The Gambler's Fate, or the Road to Ruin*)[1] in Scenes I and II. This habit of numbering the scenes became common in the earliest years of the twentieth century, and until at least 1904 it was customary to present a story-film like a stage play in this respect. From then on the practice was very gradually dropped, and scenic change was incorporated in the film without specific mention. This was probably more than an alteration in cataloguing arrangement, and indicated a gradual change of attitude. The borrowed stage technique—the vaudeville artist who made his bow before the camera, the ingenuous presentation of ventriloquists and quick-change artists by a medium which robbed their acts of meaning—were by this time dying out and a new way of telling a story, peculiar to the cinema, was slowly emerging.

It is easy to see how the idea of a change of scene would dawn on an early film producer. The 50-foot actuality or topical was frequently too short to cover an interesting subject, and the habit grew up of taking a series of films of the same subject. As it became possible to use longer strips of films the question of whether these different films were presented as a "set" or as one strip containing different scenes was decided solely by the producer's or exhibitor's convenience. To apply the principle to made-up films was a fairly obvious step, however, and followed without much delay. But to introduce a change of camera-position within the scenes was an altogether more advanced concept, and does not seem to have become really general in this period, although a few clear examples can be found in the catalogues (e.g. R. W. Paul's *Battery of Quick-Firing Guns in Action* from the Army Film, September 1900, and his *Britain's Welcome to her Sons* of about 1899–1900). *Welshed, a Derby Day Incident* (May 1903), directed by Alfred Collins, is almost unique in opening with a panning shot.[2] Apart from these isolated and probably fortuitous examples, it seems that the introduction of different shots crept in incidental to the interpolated close-up. Close-ups which were not interpolated but occupied the whole film first appeared exceedingly early in this country,

[1] See p. 96.   [2] See p. 31–2 for reference to mobile camera in made-up films.

which is considered by one authority[1] to have been the pioneer in this extremely important development of cinema technique. R. W. Paul's *Twins' Tea Party*, dating from not later than August 1898, was the forerunner of a long series of "facial expression" films (see p. 75), made chiefly by Paul himself, Hepworth, and G. A. Smith. The close-up was used almost solely for trick or comedy effects in these films, for which there was a vogue about 1900–2. J. Williamson's famous *A Big Swallow* (1903),[2] in which a man's face comes nearer and nearer until the screen is entirely covered by his open mouth, was some three years later than a film of Paul's in which exactly the same idea was actually interpolated in a film (*The Haunted Curiosity Shop*), but Paul's lead does not seem to have been maintained. The pioneer of the interpolated close-up was almost certainly G. A. Smith, who, always a scientist rather than an artist, hardly seems to have been aware of its significance. In several conversations with the author, he brushed aside his remarkable work in this connection, in order to discuss his scientific achievements and trick photography, which he apparently considered of far greater interest and importance. *Grandma's Reading Glass* (early summer 1900)[3] shows first Grandma sitting reading, and then several objects seen through her magnifying glass. This was the first of a series which continued for several years (*The Little Doctor*, May 1901;[4] *At Last! That Awful Tooth*, July 1902,[5] etc.). M. Sadoul appears to believe that the practice was not followed by other producers, but towards the close of this period examples, although still rare enough to merit special attention in the catalogues, are found in films of other makes (e.g. Gaumont's *The Runaway Match, or Marriage by Motor*, between July and August 1903, and their *The Life of a Racehorse*, between November 1903 and October 1904; Cricks and Sharp's *The Young Photographer*, not later than 1904,[6] and Hepworth's *The Glutton's Nightmare* of 1901 which includes a close-up of a steaming dish of stew).

Plagiarism of ideas was the law of the day. Once a view or an idea became popular with an audience it became popular with directors for obvious reasons. From the beginning the screens were filled with trains entering stations, fire brigades "turning-out" and other simple actualities.

---

[1] Georges Sadoul, "Early Film Production in England," *Hollywood Quarterly*, April 1946.
[2] See p. 75. [3] See p. 76. [4] See p. 76. [5] See p. 77. [6] See p. 91.

It was an easy move from watching trains enter stations to enjoying "phantom-rides" with cameras placed on the front of engines rounding curves and entering tunnels. All the main news items (royal events, racing events, etc.) were covered by all the producers. When trick films became fashionable the same tricks were repeated by everyone. Comic facial expression items appear in the catalogues of Smith, Williamson, Paul and Hepworth alike. Even Lumière's *Watering the Gardener* was copied by Smith (*Gardener with Hose, or the Mischievous Boy*), and the Black and White comedy theme was constantly recurring: Williamson (*Washing the Sweep*, 1899,[1] and Smith (*The Miller and the Sweep; The Baker and the Sweep*, 1898), Paul (*Whitewash and Miller*, 1898), and even Haggar (*The Rival Painters*)[2] as late as 1905. A remarkable example is *Burlesque of Popular Composers*, where an almost identical film was made by both Paul and Williamson. And Hepworth's *Macaroni Competition* of 1899 was faithfully followed by Gaumont's *Pie Eating Competition* of summer 1902, and that again by Paul's *Pie Eating Contest* of 1903.

Apart from some of the work of Cecil Hepworth, originality of theme and treatment was rarely the aim of our early directors. They were content to give "fine examples of already popular subjects." In their catalogues they acclaimed the virtues of their films in terms such as "clear and sharp," "very animated," "most ludicrous," and so on. Films are praised on the score that "expressions are clearly shown," or "an excellent view is obtained of their faces." "Artistic" costume dramas, adaptations of books and plays, films in which the actors were named, new ideas—these appeared from time to time, particularly from about 1904 onwards, and particularly in Gaumont films (for ambitious presentations) and the work of Hepworth (for originality). In general the only actors who were given specific credit were the vaudeville artistes, while the only new ideas thought worthy of welcome were the "tricks"; artistic pretensions were slight.

[1] See p. 88.   [2] See p. 89.

CHAPTER TWO

The Main Types of British Film

1896–1906

(I) ACTUALITIES

Movement, without topical or dramatic interest, provided the necessary thrill to bring the first film audiences together. They were satisfied to see any simple scene from everyday life reproduced on the screen. Favourite subjects were railway scenes, fire engines "turning-out," waves breaking on the seashore, street scenes, beach scenes, and so on. Typical are the examples from the work of the Brighton producers G. Albert Smith and James Williamson:

G. A. SMITH. *Waves and Spray*. Fine effect. Rough sea dashing against stone groyne. (Cat. 1898. Not later than August, 1898.)

J. WILLIAMSON. *Bank Holiday at the Dyke*. Swing boats (28 ft.), Merry-go-round (25 ft.), Cycle Railway (16 ft.), and Switch-back (46 ft.). Four separate subjects on one film (or separately). (Cat. September 1902. Not later than 1899). (115 ft.)

Hepworth was producing actualities as late as 1903.

C. HEPWORTH. *Breaking Waves*. Of all the myriads of subjects which have come within the ken of the cinematographic lens, none is more beautifully shown than the breaking waves on the sea-shore. In this picture, which was taken on an exposed portion of the coast during a gale, wave after wave is seen rolling in towards the camera, and curling over and dashing itself into clouds of spray upon the shingle. In the distance the white-crested waves are roaring and tossing in their wild race for the shore, and ever and again a tuft is torn off by the gale and carried off in fine blinding spray. (Cat. 1906. Early 1901. (50 ft.)

After each synopsis is stated both the date of the catalogue from which it is quoted and the estimated date of its production—see Appendix 5.

C. HEPWORTH. *Snapshots at the Seaside*. It is difficult to find a more animated and amusing scene than the beach of a popular seaside resort on a Bank Holiday. A large number of different and highly amusing scenes are depicted in this film; the boats gaily sailing, the children paddling, the oyster seller, the ventriloquist, and the peripatetic sweet shop—all are shown in an amusing and pleasing manner. For the paddling scenes—in which children of an older growth take part with as much pleasure as the little ones—our reporter engaged a cart to take him through the surf right into the thick of the excitement. (Cat. 1906. Latter half of 1903). (100 ft.)

Railways were a favourite subject.

C. HEPWORTH. *Express Trains*. A photograph taken in a picturesque Railway Cutting in Surrey. During the period of the picture no less than three Express Trains rush through, emitting dense clouds of steam as they pass. The trains come from the extreme distance of the view right up into the close foreground, and the effect of their rapid travelling is very fine and quite exciting. (Cat 1906. Early 1898). (50 ft.)

R. W. PAUL. *The London Express*. A G.N.R. Express dashing past Wood Green, the engine coming directly down upon the spectator at close range, producing a thrilling effect. (Cat. 1902. Before August 1898). (40 ft.)

Other directors, such as Williamson, exploited the cinematic qualities of trains, anticipating films which some fifty years later were to make magnificent use of the same material (*Nightmail, La Bête Humaine, Brief Encounter*). Cameras were attached to the trains themselves to produce phantom-rides, like those which are a motif, as it were, in *La Bête Humaine:*

WARWICK TRADING COMPANY. *Down Exeter Incline*. Taken from the buffers of an engine on the L. and S.W. Ry., leaving Queen Street Station, travelling down Exeter incline, meeting a train coming up which has an engine at either end on account of the steep ascent, plunging into Exeter Tunnel, emerging therefrom on to the curves beyond, and giving an attractive view of the scenery about. Then, after crossing and re-crossing the "points" incidental to the junction of this line with the Great Western, the train enters St. David's Station and brings the picture to an end. (Cat. April 1901. May 1898). (150 ft.)

C. HEPWORTH. *View from an Engine Front—Shilla Mill Tunnel:* A "Phantom Ride" taken at sixty miles an hour, affording a panoramic representation of some of the most beautiful of the Devonshire scenery, besides a rapid passage through the tunnel. A weird and exciting subject. (By permission of the London and South-Western Railway Co.). (Cat. 1906. Before January 1900). (50 ft.)

Other early "thrillers" include the innumerable fire brigade films:

R. W. PAUL. *Glasgow Fire Brigade.* In this film the horses are seen being harnessed to the engines, as the latter are brought out by the firemen. The engines are driven rapidly past the camera, followed by a car full of firemen, and a crowd of excited people. (100 ft.) The above engines and men driving rapidly to the fire, through High Street. At the end of picture a country cart blocks the road, with amusing effect. ((40 ft.)

Sensational Fire Engine Collision. Showing six machines, the last of which collides with the camera, producing a most astounding effect. (Cat. 1902 Probably 1898.) (55 ft.)

This is an interesting anticipation of the sensationalism of crashes and accidents which are a staple part of commercial film entertainment. The cinema was discovering its legitimate thrills early.

Comedy was frequently introduced by choosing obviously funny subjects like attempts on the greasy pole. Smith, Paul, Williamson and Hepworth all list greasy-pole films. Williamson and Hepworth both filmed lady cyclists at a period when they were still sensational.

J. WILLIAMSON. *Greasy Pole.* The film shows seven attempts to take flag from end, two of which are successful. A most amusing film shown backwards. (Cat. 1899. Before September 1899.)

C. HEPWORTH. *Egg and Spoon Race for Lady Cyclists.* This picture opens with a view of an open field on which are seen to be placed at regular intervals in a straight line a number of eggs. At a signal a bevy of ladies ride in on their bicyles, dismount at the line of eggs, and commence the difficult task of picking them up in the spoons with which each lady is provided. They then remount with one hand while holding the egg balanced in the other, and ride on to the winning post. (Cat. 1906. 1898.) (50 ft.)

The cinema interview appeared early:

WARWICK TRADING COMPANY. *Animated Portrait—Miss Marie Lloyd.*[1] Taken at the entrance of the Alhambra Theatre of Varieties, Brighton. Miss Lloyd comes out of the theatre towards the road, and a

---

[1] Taken by G. A. Smith.

friend, driving past in a dog-cart, returns and comes to meet her, when they go into the theatre together. (Cat. April 1901. May 1898.)

WARWICK TRADING COMPANY. *Miss Ellen Terry at Home.*[1] A charming half-length portrait of the popular actress. She appears at the casement window of her country cottage, kisses her hand, throws a flower, etc. Beautifully sharp and clear. (Cat. April 1901. January 1900).

In general it might be said that every producer began by making actualities by the score. Hepworth seems to have remained faithful to them to a later date than the other producers: they have almost disappeared from the new section to Williamson's catalogue of 1902, while in Paul's catalogue of the same year actualities are giving place to films of the more topical or "interest" type. Hepworth however was still producing them at the same time as his much more advanced story films.

In the same category as "actualities" should be classed the showman's local subjects, when they genuinely made them. Some touring showmen found it paid to pretend to the public that they would include local scenes in the shows given in the place they were visiting. They would tour round for advertising purposes ostentatiously cranking a camera in which there was no film at all. This was the exception rather than the rule, however, and it must remain a comfort now to those who honestly exposed their film as they turned the handle to know that their work would come to be classified fifty years later as a contribution to the early actualities.

(2) INTEREST FILMS

There is no definite division between the simple actuality film and the interest picture. The distinction at first lies chiefly in emphasis, when attention is drawn to the subject of the picture rather than to the picture itself. The fascination of the subject in its own right appears in Paul's descriptions of two films in his catalogue of August 1898.

R. W. PAUL. *Cory.* View of an enormous steam floating derrick, coaling several steamers at once. This is a panoramic picture taken from a tug which moves entirely round the vessels. (Cat. August 1898. By August 1898.) (40 or 80 ft.)

R. W. PAUL. *Monorail.* A picture of the fastest railway in the world, invented by Mr. F. B. Behr, at Tervueren, consisting of a single rail, in

[1] Taken by G. A. Smith.

which the car is seen rushing towards the spectators at the rate of 120 miles an hour. (Cat August 1898. By August 1898.) 40 ft.)

The beginning of the film of explanation, the film as a demonstration of processes in actual life, can be seen clearly in Williamson's important *Country Life* Series which appears in his catalogue of September, 1899. He describes the Series as 'perfectly natural Country Scenes, mostly illustrating simple farming operations, without any make-up or pre-arranged incident. Much appreciated by cultivated audiences." Subjects in the Series include:

J. WILLIAMSON. *Blacksmiths at work—Tyring a Cartwheel.* Shows three men hard at work at this operation. The red-hot rim is carried in and placed on the wooden framework and hammered on; afterwards water is poured on the hot rim to cool it. A busy scene, showing fine smoke and steam effect.

Seed-threshing. Shows a method of threshing turnip seed prevalent in Sussex. A large spread of stout canvas on the field forms a floor upon which is strewn the haulm to be threshed. A horse and roller is led round and round, while the men, with forks, shake up the straw, afterwards pitching it away to the side while the seed left upon the floor is swept up, and, after being winnowed, shovelled into sacks. A curious kind of tipping sledge, it will be noticed, is employed to bring the haulm to the threshing floor. (Cat. September 1899. Not later than September 1899.)

This is an embryonic documentary, although it is obvious that these first examples of picture-series of scenes from actuality are no more than a number of actuality shots grouped together on the assumption that the subject is worth more than one scene. In other words, the interest film developed out of showing several simple actualities which were related merely because they dealt with the same subject.

On September 18, 1900, Paul's important *Army Life, or How Soldiers are Made* was shown at the Alhambra. This was a series of about twenty films which, Paul claimed, were intended "to illustrate the life and career of a soldier, and the work of each branch of the Service." Facilities had been granted by Sir Evelyn Wood, Adjutant-General, to make the film possible, and Paul issued an impressive illustrated brochure advertising the Series of "Animatograph Pictures"; in an introduction dated October

1900, Paul explains that the War Office authorities foresaw that recruiting might well be stimulated by exhibition of the films. Titles include:

> Joining the Army
> Life at the Regimental Depot
> Firing at the Ranges
> Incidents of Camp Life
> Cavalry Exercises
> Royal Army Medical Corps
> Quick-Firing Guns

The catalogue quotes the Press reviews from *The Times*, *Morning Post*, *Daily News*, *Daily Mail* and many other papers. The *Echo* reports:

It is doubtful whether the Animatograph has ever before been turned to such good account. . . . Of exceptional merit combining art and actuality.

The films made no attempt to deal with any men individually as characters: the treatment was in fact actuality scenes from various aspects of Army life assembled into a series.

Also in 1900 Cecil Hepworth made two similar series, *The British Army* and *The British Navy*. These included such titles as:

> Tent Pegging Competition
> March Past of Mounted Dragoons
> Jack on the Parallel Bars
> Bluejackets Skirmishing
> "Curtain Picture"—Unfurling Sail

Hepworth concentrated most of his attention on the naval films.

By this time the idea of interpreting or explaining the subjects derived from actuality had become customary. The more important producers provide examples:

R. W. PAUL. *A Collier's Life*. An entertaining series of pictures showing a miner's life, and how the coal is won and despatched from the colliery. Scenes: Finding Matches; Holing; Loaded Tubs at Pit Mouth; Sifting; Lunch Time. (Cat. 1906. 1904.) (315 ft.)

R. W. PAUL. *Jam Making*. A series of pictures taken at Histon, near Cambridge, by courtesy of Messrs. Chivers and Sons, Ltd. A number of women and girls in clean white aprons picking currants in one of the many plantations, then weighing in the fruit is seen. As the workers are paid by results, there is great competition as to who can pick the most per day.

Arrival of the fruit at the factory. The jam boilers at work. Potting by women. Panoramic view of labelling room with large number of women finishing off the various kinds of jam. The jam covers are seen to be very quickly and neatly put on in a somewhat close view of all the operators. Concluding with two pretty children having a private entertainment with a pot of their favourite jam—strawberry. (Cat. 1906. 1906) (230 ft.)

C. HEPWORTH. *A Day with the Hop Pickers.* Many thousands of workers from the great City of London migrate annually to the Kentish hop-fields for the hop-picking, which to them is a very welcome holiday and often a substantial addition to their income. This film gives an interesting insight into the day's work of the hop-pickers. It opens with a panoramic view of a large hop-garden, partially picked, showing the people at work gathering the curious green flowers. Then we get a closer view of the various processes which constitute the day's work. The hop plants are torn and cut down from the strings which have afforded them support during their season's growth. The plants are then seized upon by a family of workers surrounding a "bin" and the flowers deftly picked from the stems. Here we have a number of most interesting snapshots of all sorts and conditions of hop-pickers at work; an old man and woman with numerous grandchildren control one bin. At another is a young and pretty girl; and at a third some East-end coster women, plain of face but sharp of wit. Three tiny children, dirty and dishevelled, sit on the ground and imitate their elders by trying to pick the flowers from a bunch of hops, and their grimaces and antics are extemely funny. Next we see a family of pickers carrying their bin into a fresh and unpicked portion of the garden, and then the measuring party come round and with a big basket measure out the hops into the bags or "pokes" in which they are stored. The number of bushels in the bin is counted and entered upon a card, which is handed to the picker, and the sacks full of hops are laid along the roadway to be gathered up by the carts at the end of the day. In another section we see these carts coming along and collecting the big bags, which they carry away to the "oast-houses," where the hops are further treated during the night. The film is of excellent quality and much beauty, and the facial expressions of these workers from London's lowest slums—out for their holiday in the fresh country—are often exceedingly ludicrous. The picture is of a quite unusual character, and is fascinating in its beauty and peculiar interest. (Cat. 1906. 1903–4.) (275 ft.)

The Story of a Piece of Slate. This picture shows the complete history of a block of slate, from the time that it is hewn from the solid rock until it is neatly packed in a railway truck ready to be delivered to the builder. In the opening of the picture there is a pretty view of the tunnel-like entrance to one of the "levels" leading to the underground slate workings. A battered one-armed man—eloquent testimony to the dangers of slate quarrying—emerges at the head of a train of trucks; tied to his breast is a lantern, whose feeble rays have illumined his path through the tunnel. A weary-looking horse draws the train of rough trucks, on each of which one or more huge blocks of slate are packed. Each truck halts for an instant on a weighing platform in order that a rough record of the slate quarried may be kept. The train winds slowly along to the sawing sheds, and as it passes we get an excellent panoramic view of the quarry. Next we see one of the trucks tilted over and a huge block of slate, weighing several tons, is thrown to the ground. With hammer and chisel the workmen quickly split it into huge thick slabs, and these are carried away to be sawn into blocks. A big circular saw slowly cleaves its way through the slate, and then the blocks come to the hands of the splitters. These men very deftly split each block first into halves, then quarters, and then finally into thin sheets, which are used for roofing and many other purposes. The thin sheets, all jagged and uneven, are carried to the trimming sheds and placed for an instant with their rough edges against a quickly revolving knife, which, in four movements, chips each uneven slate into rectangular shape. Then the slates are carried in bundles to the trucks, into which they are loaded, and each truck as it is filled is shot rapidly down a terrifically steep incline to the lower levels, where it is taken away by railroad to the various builders' yards. The film throughout is of remarkably excellent quality, and even the interior scenes are wonderfully good. (Cat. 1906. Latter part of 1904.) (300 ft.)

A film of very great interest and importance as an early documentary dealing seriously with a social problem is Cecil Hepworth's *The Aliens' Invasion*. The synopsis describes it as follows:

C. HEPWORTH. *The Aliens' Invasion.* This is the first of a series of Political Pictures, intended to present in a graphic and convincing form the political questions of the hour which are of the highest national importance. The Alien question is shown in a manner which is both highly convincing and at the same time intensely interesting.

The first scene shows the arrival of a steamer, crowded with aliens, at the London Docks, and many of its passengers can be clearly seen. Among them is one typical alien, whose face becomes familiar as the picture progresses. On the quayside a female relative welcomes him gladly and takes him to the home—a single room—which is already shared by about

twenty others, men, women and children. This room is an exact reproduction of one in the East End actually visited by our Stage Manager,
and is typical of thousands of others. Across it from end to end are several
clothes lines, on which the occupants keep their wearing apparel, for there
is nowhere else in the room to put it. A large notice in Yiddish adorns the
door, and the furniture consists of two or three broken-down bedsteads,
each of which contains as many occupants as it will hold; others sleep
on the floor in any place where fancy dictates. It is early morning, and
the first to awake is the woman whom we have previously seen upon the
quay; she arouses the other sleepers and calls them to breakfast. Those
who are too fastidious to sleep in their clothes retire behind a bedstead
to don their working apparel. The breakfast consists of the strange viands
which are purchasable in the neighbourhood of Petticoat Lane for very
small money. These are the people who oust the honest British toiler from
his work and *this* their manner of living. . . . (Cat. 1906. Latter part of
1905.)

The rest of this 450 foot film (running time 7½ minutes approximately)
then develops into a tragic story of an English workman in great need who
fails to obtain work owing to the influx of cheap foreign labour. Another
interesting political film, a kind of acted cartoon or extravaganza, shows
Hepworth's interest in exploring new subjects for film expression. It is
called *The International Exchange.*

HEPWORTH MANUFACTURING COMPANY. *The International Ex-
change.* This is a political cartoon showing clearly and forcibly the dis-
advantages which poor old-fashioned John Bull has to submit to owing
to his want of foresight. John Bull, armed with his wares, is seen trying
to trade with America, Germany, Russia and France; he knocks at their
closed door, but before gaining admittance has to pay heavy toll. All this
while representatives from these countries are entering and re-entering
the open door of Great Britain and dumping down their goods at will.
At last, however, John Bull awakes from his stupor with a violent start,
and realizing his isolated position, he decides in favour of FAIR TRADE,
and slams his door. When next America carts her ever-increasing products
to Great Britain, she receives a severe shock, and greatly excited at the turn
events have taken, spreads the news to her sister protectionists. Brisk
business is done, as each country bringing goods pays Tariff, and John
Bull raises his head, proud to meet his comrades once more on equal
ground. The picture closes with a view of India and Canada linking arms
and rejoicing together. (Cat. 1906. Latter part of 1905.) (275 ft.)

Hepworth's work consistently shows a maturity of imagination which puts it in a different category from that of any other British producer of the period. It is possible, however, to trace occasional indications of a later more advanced technique in films of other makes. The scientific films of the Charles Urban Trading Company, for example, are clearly the predecessors of the *Secrets of Nature* films of the twenties. The Urban series *Natural History*, *Unseen World* and *Marine Studies* were filmed by F. Martin-Duncan, the first two being first shown at the Alhambra on August 17, 1903. The *Unseen World* series consisted of some twenty films of between 50 and 150 feet, taken by means of the "Urban-Duncan Micro-Bioscope," which magnified the subject from "2,200,000 to 76,000,000 times." The titles themselves indicate the sort of subject filmed—*Birth of a Crystal*, *Cheese Mites*, *Circulation of Protoplasm in the Waterweed*, *Circulation of the Blood in the Frog's Foot*, *Typhoid Bacteria*, *Anatomy of the Water Flea*, etc., etc. The papers next morning were full of enthusiasm for this wonderful development, and for several years Urban continued to add new films to the series and even started "Urbanora" educational matinees for children at the Alhambra on January 9, 1905. In November of the same year an Urbanora show opened in Newcastle, the first provincial city to be visited.

Even more striking in their similarity to modern treatment and intentions are two unique sets of films, Gaumont's *Man the Lifeboat* of late 1904, and the Charles Urban Trading Company's *Borneo* series of late 1903. *Man the Lifeboat* is a set of eight films (total length 700 feet), made with the assistance of the Royal National Lifeboat Institution, telling the story of a rescue at sea in true documentary fashion. Even more curious is the similarity of the conditions under which H. M. Lomas made the *Borneo* series (1903) to the industrial sponsorship of latter-day British documentaries. The following item in *The Era*, of December 12, 1903, is of unusual interest in view of later developments:

On Tuesday evening last, at the Hotel Cecil, the North Borneo Company held their ninth annual dinner . . . After a short toast list had been run through, a series of bioscopic pictures of North Borneo, which had been photographed by Mr. H. M. Lomas, in charge of the Urban Bioscope Expedition into North Borneo, were shown, and to many people who were still unacquainted with the plantations and wonderful natural resources of that interesting country, the views and the

lecture which accompanied it proved exceedingly instructive. In this entertaining way the beautiful scenery of North Borneo and its commercial riches
were realized in a very delightful manner. . . . It occurs to us that other big
public companies who are engaged in exploring and mining operations in almost
uncivilized parts of the world would be well advised to secure the services of
the Urban Trading Company to popularize and give explanations concerning
the nature of the work carried on by them so far away from the line of vision of
anxious shareholders.

The importance of the interest film cannot be over-emphasized. Far
more than the acted farces and melodramas performed in small theatrical
sets, it represents the foundation of the true tradition of the film, and the
result is a maturity of treatment which leaves most contemporary work in
the other categories far behind.

(3) TOPICALS

The topicals, or news items, were of the greatest importance from the
first in consolidating the popularity of the film. Once the people realized
that the cinema could undertake the regular recording of events it became
recognized as an indispensable part of the public service, although in a
sense disguised always as entertainment. Only thousands could participate
in the big national events: but by means of the living representations of the
camera millions could now feel nearer to them.

The newsreels tried both the skill and the showmanship of the producer-
exhibitors. Time, then as now, became an important factor. The aim from
the first was and is to get the visual report before the public in the shortest
possible time. Barker in his lecture before the British Kinematograph
Society in February 1936, said:

All my cinema life I pinned my faith to news. Many in this room—my camera
men of old—know how I stuck to the topical. We have developed the National
coming up from Liverpool in the train. We had a luggage van turned into a dark
room with water in milk churns. Our legs soaked with developer and hypo
right through our trousers—we got swamped every time the train swung over
the points—we rushed in a hansom to our drying room to get prints made to
show the same night. Not easy when one remembers that the picture has to be
cut from about twenty cameras. I used—pre-war—to turn out some twenty-six
to thirty copies of the Derby for showing the same night, and no multiple

printer in existence. The Boat Race—from start to finish, which was several miles from our dark rooms—has been projected in Tottenham Court Road inside 1½ hours from the time of the winner passing the post, and we had no 50 to 80 m.p.h. motor-bikes in those days. I've seen Jack Smith tearing along Holborn at 8 m.p.h. in a hansom with a portion of film flying in the breeze to get it dry before reaching the Palace Theatre.

and Paul adds:

So soon as a topical film had been taken all likely purchasers were informed by telegram or post, and the dark room staff, under J. H. Martin, worked hard to turn out prints, often continuously throughout the night.

The more important news items were retained in the producers' catalogues and the showmen's repertoires, and were shown for years after they had ceased to be topical.

Favourite subjects, then as now, were the public appearances of Royalty, sports events, war news (when there was a war), launchings of ships, etc. The Derby was probably the first topical subject to be filmed in Britain. Paul filmed Persimmons' Derby of 1896, and the picture was shown at the Alhambra. When he covered the launching of H.M.S. *Albion* in 1898, he secured a scoop:

R. W. PAUL. *Disaster*. The launching of H.M.S. *Albion*, followed by the scene of the rescuing of the persons submerged in the water by the collapse of the staging. The only view of this terrible and affecting scene taken. (Cat. 1898. Not later than August 1898) (40 ft.)

Other regular sport coverages, like the Derby, were the Boat Race and Henley Regatta. Williamson had a number of films of the latter in his catalogue of September 1899. Hepworth also covered it.

C. HEPWORTH. *Arrival of Train-load of Visitors at Henley Station*. The train is literally crammed with passengers, dressed for the occasion as only visitors to Henley Regatta know how to dress. An animated and interesting study of pretty women in beautiful gowns. (Cat. 1906. 1898.) (50 ft.)

Henley Regatta—Grand Challenge Cup Race: An Early Heat. A fine representation of one of the most popular fixtures at Henley. The picture commands a splendid view of a large portion of the course quite close to the winning-post, and at the finish of the race the boats pass within a few yards of the camera. The picture gives a very good idea of the general appearance of the Regatta, besides affording an accurate representation of this important race of eight-oared boats. (Cat. 1906. 1898). (50 ft.)

Boxing matches were popular on the films. For example from Williamson's catalogue of September 1902:

J. WILLIAMSON. *Great Glove Fight.* Between Frank Lewis, champion of South of England, and Fred Gausden, champion of Sussex. Gausden beaten in three rounds. (150 ft.)

Continuation, showing the two combatants receiving the attention of their seconds, and a bookmaker paying up his calls. (Cat. September 1902. Between September 1899 and January 1901.) (80 ft.)

Car-racing is represented in Hepworth's *Progress of the Race:*

C. HEPWORTH. *Progress of the Race.* Taken at Ardskullmoat, where a fine stretch of road is seen, each car coming with terrific speed towards the camera, and causing the spectators to hold their breath as the cars swing round a very sharp corner at the speed of an express train. At another sharp dangerous turn, the road is hidden by the high banks, and it is not until the cars come round the bend at terrific speed that a view is obtained of them, and then they rush round the terrible corner—many of them skidding badly at a speed which is most exciting even in a picture. In the "Control area" at Athy, excellent close portraits of Jenatzy (Germany), the winner; and also of De Knyff (France), second, have been secured, as their respective cars are slowed up and stopped immediately in front of our camera. (Cat. 1906. June 1903.) (150 ft.)

Events connected with the Royal family produced many famous topicals. Queen Victoria's Jubilee (1897) and her funeral (1901), the Coronation of Edward VII (1902) and the Delhi Durbar (1903) provided remarkable material to help establish the historical as well as the contemporary value of the newsreel record. The Jubilee was naturally covered by every camera available: Paul's list of forty-foot films in his catalogue of August 1898 are as follows:

Sailors—Head of Procession, including blue-jackets.
Colonial—Head of Colonial procession, Canadians, etc.
Cavalcade—Royal Carriages passing Westminster.
Troops—Colonial Troops passing Westminster.
Troopers—Continuation of, and can be joined to preceding one.

Rifles—Cape Mounted Riflemen passing St. Paul's.
Dragoons—Dragoons passing St. Paul's.
Royal—Royal Carriages arriving at St. Paul's.
Royalties—Guards and escort arriving at St. Paul's.
Carriage—Queen's carriage and Indian escort arriving.
Princes—Guards and Princes. North of St. Paul's.
Queen—Queen and escort in Churchyard, showing Queen's face.

Hepworth describes his coverage of the Queen's funeral as follows:

C. HEPWORTH. *Queen's Funeral: the Procession starting from Victoria Station.* This photograph was taken from the pick of all London positions —looking straight down the station approach into the yard where the procession forms, and from such close quarters that every one who takes part in the pageant appears life-size on the screen, and has his portrait faithfully recorded. The picture is confined to the funeral cortege and the principal mourners, and a very remarkable feature about it is the splendid portrait which it includes of the King, the German Emperor, and the Duke of Connaught. They are following close behind the gun-carriage, which turns the corner right in front of the camera, so that it appears to fill the entire view. The King holds up his hand to stay the further portion of the procession for a while to allow more room to the earlier part, and while he and his companions rein up in the centre of the view, he leans over and talks to first one and then the other. The result is a most delightful animated group of the three august personages. (Cat. 1906. January 1901.) (75 ft.)

Williamson filmed the decorated streets of London from a car before the Coronation was due to take place. (It was, of course, actually postponed). Here is his description, list of streets, and footage exposed.

J. WILLIAMSON. *Coronation: Through London on Wednesday, June 25th.* While the streets were still in the full glory of the Coronation Decorations, on a Decauville Motor Car (by permission of the Motor Car Company, Ltd.). This is a splendid subject, giving the best possible idea of the gaily decorated streets, still crowded with sightseers. We are prepared to supply any length of this from 100 ft.

Bank, Mansion House, etc.	42 ft.
Cheapside	21 ft.
Ludgate Hill and Circus	38 ft.
Borough and Borough Road	28 ft.
Westminster Bridge Road, etc.	65 ft.

Whitehall and Canadian Arch	48 ft.
Trafalgar Square	48 ft.
Piccadilly	14 ft.
St. James' Street	42 ft.

(Cat. September 1902. June 1902.)

Hepworth is justly proud of his view of the procession from the Canadian Arch looking up Whitehall:

C. HEPWORTH. *The State Carriages and Prince of Wales's Procession in Whitehall.* Absolutely the finest coign of vantage on the entire route was afforded by the Canadian Arch, and our cameras occupied the most advantageous position on that structure. This picture shows the whole of the State Procession passing slowly right towards the camera, which is looking up the length of Whitehall. As practically all the state carriages are seen at one time together with the several escorts of Life Guards, etc., the beauty of the picture may be imagined. (Cat. 1906. June 1902.) (100 ft.)

Paul covered the Delhi Durbar of 1903. He describes his 240 foot film as follows:

R. W. PAUL. *The Delhi Durbar.* A superb record of one of the greatest pageants of our times. About 210 elephants with their gaily-decked howdahs and trappings were on the scene. The Viceroy and Lady Curzon, Duke and Duchess of Connaught and most of the Ruling Princes of India with their many attendants took part in the procession, besides all types of Indian soldiery. (Cat. 1906. January 1903) (240 ft.)

The South African War (October 1899 to May 1902) greatly stimulated the development of the newsreel. It was covered by the British Mutoscope and Biograph Company,[1] by Urban and Paul whose agents visited the scene of battle behind the lines. John Bennett Stanford was the first man to make war newsreels, not Joe Rosenthal as it is commonly claimed.[2] He was the son of a wealthy family in Brighton, and took up kinematography as a hobby. When the South African War broke out he wanted G. A. Smith to equip him, but Smith sent him to Prestwich,[3] from whom he bought an amount of expensive equipment. He went out to South Africa and sent back three negatives—of such subjects as digging trenches and crossing rivers. G. A. Smith sent these to Urban, who showed them at

---

[1] *The Biograph in Battle*, by W. K. L. Dickson.   [2] See p. 26.
[3] Equipment manufacturer.

the Alhambra, where they aroused great enthusiasm among the audience. But Stanford did not send any more material, and this led Urban to send Rosenthal and others out as his camermen. It was Rosenthal who sent home the first action picture, and he may rightly be called the first professional war cameraman.

WARWICK TRADING COMPANY. *A Skirmish with the Boers near Kimberley by a Troop of Cavalry Scouts Attached to General French's Column.* One of the liveliest scenes yet photographed in three views.

    I. The Scouts in pursuit of the Boers.
    II. Bringing the Maxims into Action.
    III. A Charge and General Fusilade.

These scenes portray one of the many brushes with the Boers by a contingent of General French's Army during his march to relieve Kimberley. Several kopjes in the background. (Photographed by Mr. J. Rosenthal, of our War Staff).

These pictures produce a stereoscopic effect, and the clear atmosphere gives it a tremendous depth, enabling one to see the thousands of troops in the distance, fighting at the base of a kopje, while the dust arising from the galloping cavalry lends further realism to this splendid subject. (Cat. April 1901. 1899–1900.) (150 ft.)

Many scenes were of course taken at home, obviously, covering the departure and return of troops. The following are examples of these films:

WARWICK TRADING COMPANY. *The "Braemar Castle" Leaving for South Africa.* This view was procured as the *Braemar Castle* gradually leaves the Docks and full face portraits of the various officers and troops aboard ship was procured. As these troops were some of the first to leave England for South Africa, there are many smiling countenances herein portrayed who we regret to state since met with misfortune. (Cat. April 1901. October 1899.)

C. HEPWORTH. *C.I.V.'s Marching Aboard s.s. "Garth Castle."* An excellent photograph showing the first detachment of the City of London Imperial Volunteers (the Lord Mayor's Own) stepping aboard the ship which is to convey them to the seat of war. By kind permission, this photograph was taken from a commanding position on the deck of the vessel, just facing the gangway over which the Volunteers pass. The men pass so close that every face is an actual portrait, and every detail of their uniform is plainly visible. (Cat. 1906. January 1900.) (75 ft.)

Other films were taken in Africa, usually well out of the firing line.

WARWICK TRADING COMPANY. *The Surrender of Kroonstad to Lord Roberts, May* 12, 1900. Showing Lords Roberts and Kitchener with Staff Officers entering Kroonstad at the head of the Mounted Column of Foreign Attaches, Bodyguard and Waggonnette, in which are seated the Landrost and other Officials who went out to surrender the Town to Lord Roberts. As the Column slowly files into the Town and by our Camera, magnificent portraits of all were secured. Lord Kitchener is mounted on a White Charger (with Indian officer riding beside him), on the right of Lord Roberts, and Sir John Hill Johnes, V.C., on the left of the Commander-in-Chief. (Cat. April 1901. May 1900.) (150 ft.)

R. W. PAUL. *The Royal Engineers' Balloon.* In a deep ravine on the road from Johannesburg to Pretoria, is seen the Balloon Section of the Royal Engineers with their wagons, coming towards the spectator. The balloon itself, which is hitched to the wagon, gives a fine effect, as it approaches the spectator until it almost fills the picture. This is entirely a novel subject in war films, and being sharp and clear is sure to be well received. (Cat. 1902. c. 1900.) (60 ft.)

R. W. PAUL. *Cronje's Surrender to Lord Roberts.* This historical film which is the only one of the subject taken, shows Cronje in a cart after his defeat at Paardeberg, followed by an escort of C.I.V. As the cart passes the camera, Cronje is seen to look out in astonishment at it. The picture is most successful, considering the circumstances under which it was taken in the early morning. (Cat. 1902. February 29, 1900.) (60 ft.)

Peace was celebrated by Hepworth in a film called *Peace with Honour.*

C. HEPWORTH.   *Peace with Honour*
                              An Allegorical Picture

NOTE.—The above picture partly consists of excerpts from some of our famous topical films, but by far the larger portion is quite new.

This picture is opened by a vociferous newsboy who proclaims Peace both vocally and by his contents bill. In a moment we see a madly excited crowd rushing to hear the joyful tidings. Next we get glimpses of those who have been principally instrumental in bringing the war to so satisfactory a conclusion. First is seen a splendid portrait of Lord Roberts entering his carriage; then we see Lord Milner as taken when he last returned to England. This is followed by a representative crowd of C.I.V.'s who did such yeoman service in the war, and then comes an allegorical

67

representation of the Conclusion of Peace, and of Britain's gratitude to Lord Kitchener. On a marble dais there is a group of British flags guarded by a "gentleman in Khaki" with a big Union Jack. Britannia enters, and drawing aside a central flag, discloses a fine portrait of Lord Kitchener, whereat the soldier cheers lustily. Britannia offers up a laurel wreath to Britain's hero, and she then leads in a conquered and dispirited Boer. The Briton shakes him heartily by the hand, and the Boer, pleased and pacified, sits down beside him on the dais, and smokes the "pipe of peace" with his late enemy. The picture closes with Britannia smiling approval on the two—now the firmest of friends. May so end all Great Britain's wars. (Cat. 1906. Early summer, 1902.) (100 ft.)

By far the best and most important genuine war films were made under Charles Urban's direction by operators of first the Warwick Trading Company (Joe Rosenthal, John Bennett Stanford, E. M. Hyman, Sydney Goldman—see p. 26) and later the Charles Urban Trading Company (Joe Rosenthal, C. Rider Noble, George Rogers—see pp. 17, 18). But before leaving the subject of topical films, the now famous "faked" news films should be mentioned. War pictures taken behind the lines where it was possible to operate the heavy camera equipment were not exciting enough for a public reading front line reports in the Press. A number of producers therefore reconstructed front line events at home. Paul, the Sheffield Photo Company, Gaumont, Mitchell and Kenyon, and Williamson all made these films as Dramatic Representations of Current Events. Mitchell and Kenyon made *The Dispatch Bearer* (120 feet), a British dispatch bearer fighting his way through a crowd of Boers.[1] Paul called his films *Reproductions of Incidents of the Boer War* ("arranged under the supervision of an experienced military officer from the front.") Here are examples:

R. W. PAUL. *Bombardment of Mafeking*. The British soldiers are sitting round the camp fire. Several shells explode near them, causing much amusement. (Cat. 1902. After October, 1899). (60 ft.)

Nurses on the Battlefield. A most affecting picture, but very beautiful and natural. It depicts the battlefield with the wounded and dead scattered over it. The picture shows the stretcher party with doctor and his orderly, who, with the nurses, are tending a wounded Boer. At the same time a British soldier is carried down by his comrades to the other nurses. *Specially recommended*. (Cat. 1902. After October 1899.) (60 ft.)

[1] Bromhead. B.K.S. Lecture, p. 8 (December 11, 1935).

The Gaumont Company "faked," among other subjects, the *Signing of the Peace at Vereeniging in* 1902. Colonel A. C. Bromhead describes the making of this film as follows:

Our little picture, which was ludicrously imaginative, showed actors posing as Lord Kitchener, Lord Milner, and the British staff with the Boer leaders— President Steyn, Smuts, Botha, de Wet, and others discussing dramatically and finally signing the Peace conditions. We included Lord Roberts and only found out afterwards that he had not been there.[1]

The Boer War was not the only subject for "faking." Bromhead continues:

Many other sensational staged topicals were made. The assassination of King Alexander and Queen Draga of Serbia, in 1903, was produced in a short, but meaty film. This was confined chiefly to the Fair Ground Shows for exhibition. —it was a bloodthirsty piece of work, omitting no details.

Then there was a very effective film portraying the eruption of Mt. Pelee, and the destruction of St. Pierre, Martinique, in the year 1902, when the whole town was destroyed in ten minutes. Two or three did this—I think Pathé's was the best. It was an ingenious picture of models and firework display—the forerunner of the fine model work of to-day.[1]

The Sheffield Photo Company made a film of the Russo-Japanese War:

SHEFFIELD PHOTO COMPANY. *Russo-Japanese War—Attack on a Japanese Convoy.* A party of Cossacks is seen chasing a Coolie Spy, from whom they endeavour to obtain information respecting a Jap Convoy. After threatening him with a pistol, the information is given and the Cossacks ride away, dragging the Coolie with them by his pigtail.

The next scene shows the Convoy with its escort hotly pursued by a Russian Patrol. Seeing escape hopeless, the Japs halt, dismount, open fire on the Cossacks, wounding one and driving the rest away for a time. Before proceeding the Japs dress the wounds of the injured Cossack and place him in the convoy waggon.

Last scene, laid in beautiful rugged scenery, shows the Convoy crossing a drift. When in mid-stream the advance rider comes in contact with a Cossack party, on whom he promptly fires, the remaining Japs ride up to his assistance and succeed in putting the Cossacks out of action. During the excitement the wounded Russian makes his escape from the waggon, but on reaching the bank he is seen and promptly shot.

[1] Lecture to the B.K.S., February 3, 1936.

The plucky Japs with the Convoy are then seen mounting the opposite bank of the river and disappear round the bend.

THIS IS WITHOUT DOUBT THE FINEST WAR FILM ON THE MARKET.

The greatest care has been exercised in producing the above picture, every detail having been considered. The Japanese, Russians, and Coolies being perfect representations. (Cat. undated, probably 1904.) (250 ft.)

The most famous of all these "faked" incidents was probably Williamson's *Attack on a China Mission*. This was filmed in his own garden.

J. WILLIAMSON. *Attack on a China Mission.* The scene opens with the outer gate of the premises; a Chinaman with flourishing sword approaches and tries the gate. Finding it fastened he calls the others, who come rushing up; one leaps over the gate, and the combined attack results in forcing it open: nine Boxers in Chinese costumes of varied character now swarm in, stopping occasionally to fire in the direction of the house.

The second scene shows the front of the house—the missionary walking in front with a young lady; wife and child are seated a little way further off. At the first alarm the missionary drops his book and sends the young lady into the house to fetch rifle and pistol; then rushes to his wife and child and sees them safely into the house; takes cover behind some bushes, discharges his revolver at the Boxers advancing in different directions, kills one, then picks up rifle and discharges it at another; his ammunition exhausted, he comes to close quarters with another Boxer armed with a sword, and, after an exciting fight, is overcome, and left presumably killed. Meanwhile others of the attacking party have closed round the young lady and followed her, retreating into the house.

Missionary's wife now appears waving handkerchief on the balcony; the scene changes and shows party of bluejackets advancing from the distance, leaping over a fence, coming through the gate, kneeling and firing in fours, and running forward to the rescue, under command of a mounted officer.

The fourth scene is a continuation of the second. The Boxers are dragging the young lady out of the house, which they have set on fire, at the moment the bluejackets appear; a struggle takes place with the Boxers; mounted officer rides up and carries off the young lady out of the mêlée.

The missionary's wife now rushes out of the house pointing to the balcony, where she has left her child; a bluejacket has secured it, but his passage down the stairs being blocked, three sailors mount on each other's shoulders and land the child safely in the mother's arms. The struggle with the Boxers continues, but they are finally overcome and taken prisoners. (Cat. September 1902. January 1901.) (230 ft.)

(iv) PANORAMIC FILMS AND TRAVELOGUES

A branch of the earliest actualities soon developed into the simple scenes or panoramas of well-known places at home or overseas. It is a small stage from the view of Whitehall to the view of Paris, the Norwegian fjord or Niagara Falls from the point of view of the camera, but from the point of view of the untravelled audience the service of the motion picture to the widening of experience was immense. The enlarged moving picture gave these audiences for the first time in history a direct reproduction of the surface movement of life in other countries, and so a more vivid impression of the world than could ever be gained by still photographs or drawings of the contemporary popular periodicals. The scenes or panoramas (i.e. scenes in which the camera, either by turning on its base or being carried on a moving vehicle, included a wider view than was possible with a static camera) soon developed into short travelogues, or groups of scenes in continuity.

Paul was the first producer to distribute foreign scenes. In 1896 he sent his cameraman Harry Short to Portugal, Spain and Egypt. Although the result was mainly an exhibition of scenic photography, other subjects were included, such as records of national dances. The following are quoted from Paul's catalogue of August 1898.

Spain and Portugal—
    Madrid—Puerte del Sel.
    Lisbon—Praca do Municipie.
    Bull-fighters—Procession of.
    Andalusian Dance.

Egypt—
    Pyramids—The
    Cairo—Scene in
    Camels.

Sweden—
    Swedish National Dance. Three subjects.
    Laplanders' Village.

Constantinople—
    Scene of Armenian Massacres.
    Street in Stamboul.

The Andalusian Dance taken as early as 1897 is summarized in Paul's 1902 catalogue as follows:

R. W. PAUL. *Andalusian Dance*. Executed by two native performers, this picture, taken in Spain, is one of the few representations of unsophisticated Spanish dancing, and fully shows the grace and beauty of the movement. (Cat. 1902. 1897.) (40 ft.)

Eventually Paul covered, in addition to the countries already listed, the Holy Land, India, Switzerland and Japan. In the 1906 catalogue his Norwegian series form a continuous travelogue of over 1,000 feet (approximately ten minutes running time). Examples from the series are:

R. W. PAUL. *Laatifoss Falls*. A series of three views. The first showing the entire Fall, the second the bottom of the Fall with fine spray effect, the third being the Rapids below. (80 ft.)

Hammerfest. Panorama taken from a hill of the most northerly inhabited town in Norway—Hammerfest. Fishing smacks can be seen in the harbour, while the houses and churches stand out in stereoscopic relief. (80 ft.)

Sun. A strange and beautiful picture of the midnight sun at Scare. A magnificent cloud-laden sky is shown as a panoramic effect; the sun breaking into the picture produces a marvellous effect on the waters of the Arctic Fiords, from which it was photographed. (Cat. 1906. July 1903.) (60 ft.)

Cecil Hepworth had made many panoramas at home, but did not go abroad until 1900, when he filmed the Paris Exhibition.

C. HEPWORTH. *Panorama of the Paris Exhibition. No. 1*. This photograph was taken from a very swiftly moving steamboat travelling close by one bank of the River Seine, so that an excellent panoramic picture of the other bank is obtained. The photograph starts with the extreme end of the exhibition frontage by the Place de la Concorde, and shows several of the buildings of the Rue des Nations. The stereoscopic effect of the buildings passed is very fine. (50 ft.)

No. 2. This is a continuation of the previous picture, and shows several of the most picturesque pavilions in the Rue des Nations. At times the intervals between the buildings afford glimpses into the most distant portions of the Exhibition, and this photograph gives a good general idea of the appearance of this vast fair. (50 ft.)

No. 3. The remainder of the entire river front of the Exhibition is beautifully portrayed in this photograph. The boat passes under several of the well-known bridges erected for the purposes of the Exhibition. Buildings of all descriptions are seen; from the Eiffel Tower and the wonderful erection forming the Schneider exhibit, to the merest palace of amusement in all its wonderful tracery of design. The picture is full of movement, and marvellous stereoscopic relief is yielded by the buildings, at different distances, passing one another at varying rates. Crowds of sightseers are seen walking about, and the numerous steamboats on the river lend extra animation to the beautiful scene. (Cat. 1906. Middle of 1900.) (100 ft.)

His cameramen subsequently covered Japan, India, China, Germany and North Africa. Some of the Far Eastern films are remarkable for their early documentary approach.

HEPWORTH MANUFACTURING COMPANY. *Coaling a Battleship at Nagasaki.* Here we have the actual scene of transferring coal from a barge in the harbour of Nagasaki into a war-ship drawn up along-side. Again the method is peculiar and strange to European eyes; hundreds of Japanese women, rapidly scrambling in the barge, fill innumerable little baskets with coal and pass them very quickly from hand to hand until they are finally tipped into the bunkers of the ship and pitched back empty into the barge. The scene is all bustle and orderly haste, and it is easy to imagine that even with this crude method of coaling a large quantity may be shipped in a comparatively short time. (Cat. 1906. Between June 1903 and June 1904.) (50 ft.)

As in the case of interest and scientific films, the most important work of the period in connection with travel films was that sponsored by Charles Urban (see pp. 17 and 25). Apart from the films of G. A. Smith and J. Williamson, almost all the films made for the Warwick Trading Company (and after 1902, for the Charles Urban Trading Company), were in some measure educational, dealing with either scientific or travel subjects. The films taken by Rosenthal in the Philippines (1901), F. B. Stewart in India (1901), J. H. Avery in Morocco (1901) and F. Ormiston-Smith in the Alps (1902) were all made for the Warwick Trading Company. Rosenthal and Ormiston-Smith went with Urban to his new company, and made *Living Canada* (Rosenthal, early 1903), and *The Wintry Alps* and *Picturesque Switzerland* (1903), *Winter Sports Series* (early 1904) and *Northern Ice*

Sports (c. 1905), all made by Ormiston-Smith. Dr. J. Gregory Mantle made an Indian Series in 1903, and in 1904 H. M. Lomas made the *North Borneo* series mentioned elsewhere (see p. 60).

Whether taken at home or overseas, the scale on which the travel scenes, panoramas and travelogues were produced showed that British film-makers realized that the mobile camera was fulfilling its proper function in recording these pictures, as it was in the case of actualities and topicals. These films are the ones which are most full of interest to us seeing them some fifty years later. They form the first chapter in the recording of history in the motion picture, and for this reason alone those prints that have survived will be treasured and preserved and reprinted for future generations of students.

(v) VAUDEVILLE

With the films of this section we turn to the other branch of cinema, the recording not of actuality but of artifice. The filming of vaudeville turns was the simplest form of artificial film subject. Historically it is interesting because the vaudeville artists filmed were frequently well-known performers, and were consequently the first named players in the history of motion pictures. Their work, as an item in a film programme, was quite natural when we remember that these films were first shown either as a collective "turn" in a music-hall or as a separate show in a fairground.

Paul specialized in filming these turns. Perhaps it is noteworthy that Hepworth never produced any. Films were made of artistes singing comic songs (many of them with records to accompany them), of knockabout comedians, of trick cyclists, acrobats, manipulators of American clubs, conjurers and dancers. Paul also photographed marionettes.

Examples from Paul's catalogue are:

R. W. PAUL. *Devant's Hand-Shadows.* Shadowgraphy is always popular at entertainments for young and old, but few artistes have worked it up to the perfection here seen. Some of Mr. Devant's more original and popular ideas are shown in the film, which is so done as to give the same effect on the screen as if the performer himself were at work. (80 ft.)

Chirgwin, The "White-eyed Kaffir." The music-hall favourite is shown in his most familiar oddities. He appears in an enormous hat, and, divesting himself of this and his fantastic coat, on which the white hand appears, seats himself. He takes a tray and two tobacco pipes which he causes to execute a hornpipe, accompanying them by amusing gesticulation. (80 ft.)

Mr. Maskelyne (of the Egyptian Hall), Spinning Plates and Basins. This little scene shows a piece of juggling by this famous master of the art. Taking a number of common plates and bowls, he starts them spinning together, and, while they rotate, marshals them like soldiers on the table. Their evolutions, under the occasional touch of his trained hand, are truly wonderful. (40 ft.)

Mel B. Spurr gives "The Village Blacksmith." This well-known society entertainer makes a speciality of funny facial expression. He is seen acting the above song in dumb show, and when the appropriate music is played to accompany the picture the effect is very laughable. (Cat. 1902. 1897.) (60 ft.)

This last example shows the interest the first film-makers had in "facial expressions," which became a branch of the vaudeville film in its own right. Everyone, including Hepworth, produced "facials."

G. A. SMITH. *Comic Faces.* Old man drinking glass of beer, old woman taking snuff. Two subjects on one film. (Cat. 1898. Not later than September, 1898.) (75 ft.)

J. WILLIAMSON. *A Big Swallow.* "I won't! I won't! I'll eat the camera first." Gentleman reading, finds a camera fiend with his head under a cloth, focussing him up. He orders him off, approaching nearer and nearer, gesticulating and ordering the photographer off, until his head fills the picture, and finally his mouth only occupies the screen. He opens it, and first the camera, then the operator disappear inside. He retires munching him up and expressing his great satisfaction. Cat. September 1902. Between January 1901 and June 1902.) (65 ft.) (This is an interesting use of the big close-up.)

R. W. PAUL. *Facial Expressions.* An actor with wigs and face paint making it understood by dumb show that he is impersonating various people, imitates a sanctimonious old man reading, then an old woman with wigs and shawl. The facial expressions are exceedingly funny. (Cat. 1906. 1902.) (80 ft.)

Funny Faces. A new series of startlingly funny facial expressions. Highly amusing. Good photographic quality. (Cat. 1906, 1904.) (55 ft.)

HEPWORTH MANUFACTURING COMPANY. *Comic Grimacer.* A human face shown the full size of the screen is always a comic and interesting sight, and when the face is of the "indiarubber" variety, and the owner can pull it about and distort it into frightful and hideous knots, the pictured result is bound to be interesting and laughable. (Cat. 1906. Between January 1901 and March 1902.) (50 ft.)

It is important to note that the first use of close-ups was for comic and not dramatic effect. The most highly developed use of the close-up is to be found in the work of G. A. Smith. In the summer of 1900 he began the production of a series of short films in which the close-up was extended from its already popular use in the "facials" to a stage which is of extraordinary significance in the history of cinema technique. These films did not consist of just a single shot, as in the case of the facials, but a general view into which was cut a close-up of some particular object. The films, which in reality contained the elements of constructive editing, were regarded at the time as "turns" for the exploitation of a single camera trick, and the following examples may conveniently be included under the heading of "Vaudeville":

WARWICK TRADING COMPANY. *Grandma's Reading Glass.* This, the first of a series of most unique pictures, was conceived and invented by us. Grandma is seen at work at her sewing-table, while her little grandson is playfully handling her reading-glass, focussing same on various objects, viz., a newspaper, his watch, the canary, grandma's eye, and the kitten, which objects are shown in abnormal size on the screen when projected. The conception is to produce on the screen the various objects as they appeared to Willy while looking through the glass in their enormously enlarged form. The big print on the newspaper, the visible working of the mechanism of the watch, the fluttering of the canary in the cage, the blinking of grandma's eye, and the inquisitive look of the kitten, is most amusing to behold. The novelty of the subject is sure to please every audience. (Cat. April 1901. Between May and August 1900.) (100 ft.)

WARWICK TRADING COMPANY. *The Little Doctor.* Children playing at "doctors" with the kitten in a cradle as patient. When the medicine is administered a magnified view of the kitten's head is shown, the manner in which the little animal receives its dose (of milk) from a spoon, being most amusing. (Cat. November 1903. Not later than May 1901.) (100 ft.)

WARWICK TRADING COMPANY. *At Last! That Awful Tooth.* A gentleman suffering with toothache, and having tried numerous remedies in vain is making frantic efforts to pull out the offending member with a piece of string. He at last succeeds, and in his delight seizes a large reading glass to view the tooth. A circular picture showing the magnified tooth as it appears through the reading glass makes a laughable finish. (Cat. November 1903. July 1902.) (50 ft.)

A development of the vaudeville branch of films was the beginning of cartoons, often associated with patriotic subjects. These films were cartoons only in the sense that artists drew their pictures rapidly whilst being photographed. Other patriotic films produced kaleidoscopes of flags, tableaux effects and further devices. Examples show best the range of these subjects.

R. W. PAUL. *Britannia.* A beautiful picture, by Mr. Charles Bertram, the Court Conjuror, who produces the flags of all nations from an apparently empty hat, welding them all together into one huge Union Jack which covers the scene, and then dropping, discloses the figure of Britannia standing by a lion. (Cat. 1898. By August 1898.) (60 ft.)

R. W. PAUL. *Political Favourites.* Suitable for all shades of politics. An artist draws large cartoons in view of the audience, showing Mr. Campbell-Bannerman, Mr. Balfour, Lord Rosebery, Duke of Devonshire, the late Sir W. Harcourt, and Mr. Chamberlain. The last two hold two loaves of same size bearing the words "Protection" and "Free Trade." (Cat. 1906. April 1904.) (150 ft.)

HEPWORTH MANUFACTURING COMPANY. *Animated Cartoon.* "*Wiping Something off the Slate.*" At the opening of this picture clouds of smoke rolling away, reveal the figure of a "gentleman in khaki" near a huge slate, on which the word "Majuba" is written, and over which the Boer flag proudly waves. The British soldier tears down this emblem, trampling it under-foot, and goes aside for a moment to fetch some water in his helmet. Then, with the bedraggled, saturated flag, he wipes the offensive word from the slate. He has just finished this, when a shell bursting near, wounds him on the temple. Almost fainting, he yet manages to bind up the wound, pick up his rifle, and to take up a position at the "ready" in the well-known pose of "The Absent-Minded Beggar." The wound, however, proves too much, and he staggers and falls just as the Union Jack floats out behind him, forming a striking background to the picture. (Cat. 1906. Early 1900). (75 ft.)

HEPWORTH MANUFACTURING COMPANY. *The International Exchange*. See back, page 59. (Cat. 1906. Latter part of 1905.) (275 ft.)

(vi) TRICK FILMS

The acknowledged pioneer and master of the trick film is Georges Méliès. He was the first to make trick films (1896), and his productions were shown in many countries, including Britain. Undoubtedly his work formed the pattern for many films made in this country, but on close inspection it seems that the influence was not all in one direction. The early date of some of G. A. Smith's films has already been mentioned (see p. 49). And the extraordinary similarity of Paul's *Voyage of the "Arctic," or How Captain Kettle Discovered the North Pole* to Méliès' *Conquest of the Pole* is interesting in view of the fact that Paul's film was made in the winter of 1903 and that of Méliès not until 1912.

G. A. SMITH. *A completely Novel Series of Films*. (Protected under the Patent Laws in Great Britain and Abroad.) New and Original Effects. No Exhibition of Animated Photographs is complete without some of these Unique Specimens of the Art. The following are now ready, and additional ones are being prepared by the inventor and patentee. (Each approximately 70–75 ft. long.)

1. *The Corsican Brothers* (from the well-known Romantic Play as produced at the Lyceum Theatre). One of the twin brothers returns home from shooting in the Corsican Mountains, and is visited by the ghost of the other twin. By special photographic contrivances the ghost appears quite transparent. After indicating that he has been killed by a sword thrust, and appealing for vengeance, he disappears. A "vision" then appears showing the fatal duel in the snow. To the Corsican's amazement, the duel and death of his brother are vividly depicted in the vision, and finally, overcome by his feelings, he falls to the floor just as their mother enters the room.

2. *Photographing a Ghost*. An amusing contrast to the foregoing; causes astonishment and roars of laughter.
Scene: A Photographer's Studio. Two men enter with a large box labelled "ghost." The photographer scarcely relishes the order, but

78

eventually opens the box, when a striking ghost of a "swell" steps out. The ghost is perfectly transparent so that the furniture, etc., can be seen through his "body." After a good deal of amusing business with the ghost, which keeps disappearing and reappearing, the photographer attacks it with a chair. The attack is amusingly fruitless, but the ghost finally collapses through the floor. A clean, sharp, and perfect film. (Cat. 1898. Not later than September 1898.)

Williamson in his catalogue of September 1899 has a single trick film, *The Clown Barber*.

> J. WILLIAMSON. *The Clown Barber*. Gentleman enters barber's shop, knocks and takes a seat. Clown enters, to evident consternation of customer, dances round, and proceeds with the shaving, using a large bowl and brush; lathers him, and then producing a huge razor, commences to shave, but the gentleman becoming alarmed, and rather restive, cuts his head off, and finishes the operation at the sideboard; puts the head on again; customer gets up, expresses his entire satisfaction at the success of the operation, pays and departs. (Cat. 1899. Not later than September 1899.) (60–75 ft.)

Paul's trick films are not announced before his catalogue of 1902, which suggests a late development of this type of work in his case. One of them, *The Magic Sword*, the synopsis of which is too long to quote, concerns a knight, a lady, a ghost, a witch, an ogre of large proportions, a battlement, a cave, an abduction of the lady by the witch, a magic cauldron, and a Good Fairy (total length 180 ft.). What is significant is Paul's statement about the film. "A sumptuously produced extravaganza in three dissolving scenes, with many novel and beautiful trick effects, now introduced for the first time. The period of this dramatic mystery is in the Middle Ages, and the facts of the actors and costumes being Old English, together with the original nature of the plot, cannot fail to please English-speaking audiences, who have become weary of foreign pictures of this class."

In his 1902 catalogue Williamson shows evidence of turning once more to trick films, producing rather stereotyped pictures such as *The Puzzled Bather and his Animated Clothes*.

> J. WILLIAMSON. *The Puzzled Bather and his Animated Clothes*. Bather approaches water, and stands considering whether he will venture; feels the water, and deciding to go in proceeds to undress; he finds some difficulty in completing that operation, for as soon as he has divested him-

self of some of his apparel, it is immediately replaced in some mysterious manner by others, until he has quite a pile beside him. Becoming exasperated at his futile efforts to undress, he plunges in clothes and all, and immediately returns to the bank relieved of these troublesome clothes. However, just as he is congratulating himself his raiment follows him out of the water, a bit at a time, and assumes its proper place on his person, until he is again fully dressed. He gives up in despair, and walks away, the clothes on the bank following. One of the funniest effects of reversing. (Cat. 1902. 1901.) (80 ft.)

Paul in his 1906 catalogue produces one of the many motoring trick films, *The ? Motorist*.

R. W. PAUL. *The ? Motorist*. A motor-car is seen at the gateway of a villa, with motorist carefully handing his lady into the car, and they drive off and soon get up a good speed. A careful policeman thinks they are exceeding the limit, and waves to them to pull up, but they decline, and he stands right in the way of the car, being caught up by the front gear, and carried away for some yards, until he is eventually dropped off, and one of the car wheels goes over him. The policeman collects the pieces of himself, and resumes his attempt to uphold the law. The motor-car then goes on, until a public-house is seen to entirely stop the way, and the policeman thinks he has now caught his prey. The car, however, does not stop, but continues its journey right up the front of the house, to the dismay of the fast assembling crowd. The car goes motoring right across the clouds, makes a friendly call on the sun, calmly circling round its circumference, then resumes its cloudy journey, and reaches the planet Saturn. The motorist continues his wild career round the highway of Saturn's ring, but eventually rides off the unusual track into space, and the car is seen falling gracefully through the clouds to earth, until it drops through the roof of a building which turns out to be a Court of Justice. Great confusion is naturally caused, though the car continues its journey unhindered out of the Court, followed by a policeman, magistrate, and other officials, but to their astonishment, while they yet look at the car, and endeavour to arrest the delinquents, a countryman's cart in place of motor, and smock-frocked man and his wife appear, and start moving off, until they get out of reach of justice, when the countryman's cart suddenly becomes again a motor, which now succeeds in making good its escape. (Cat. 1906. 1905–6.) (190 ft.)

The Dancer's Dream belongs to sentimental fantasy.

R. W. PAUL. *A Dancer's Dream*. A young ballet girl is dozing com-

17. Scientific Films

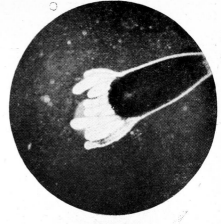

Freshwater Hydra. C.U.T.C., 1903

The Active Water Flea. C.U.T.C., 1903

The Octopus. C.U.T.C., 1903

18. News and Interest from the Far East

Execution of a Chinese Bandit
C.U.T.C., 1904

Guns outside Port Arthur. C.U.T.C., 1904

General Kuropatkin and General Mah
C.U.T.C., 1904

19. The Camera on Location

J. Rosenthal on an encampment outside
Port Arthur, 1904

Lomas at Lake Baikal, 1904

Rosenthal
ring the
uth African
r, 1901

20. The Camera on Location

Camera fixed on the front of a train

Charles Urban in Rome, 1901

Bioscopist beside ruins on the Nile

21. Topicals at Home

Funeral of Queen Victoria,
1901

Gordon-Bennett Motor Race.
C. HEPWORTH, 1903

Return of T.R.H. the
Prince and Princess of
Wales.
R. W. PAUL, 1903

Crowds on Derby Day.
C.U.T.C., 1903–4

22. Vaudeville Films —"Facials" and Close-Ups

Funny Faces. R. W. PAUL
1904

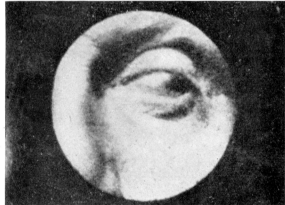

That Troublesome Collar
R. W. PAUL, 1902–3

Grandma's Reading Glass
G. A. SMITH, 1906

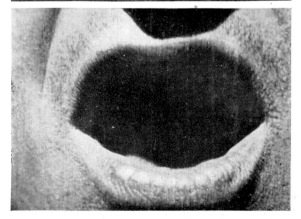

The Big Swallow
J. WILLIAMSON, 1901–2

Blue Beard

Ali-Baba

Aladdin

24. Trick Films of R. W. Paul

A Railway Collision, 1898

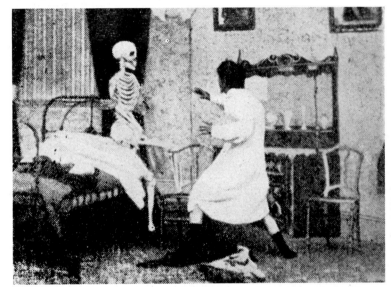

Undressing Extraordinary 1901–2

The Magic Sword, 1902

25. Comedy Films of R. W. Paul

Nursery, 1898

Come Along, Do!, 1898

The Dancer's Dream, 1905

A Curate's Dilemma, 1906

26. Other Typical Comedy Films

The Miller and the Sweep.
G. A. SMITH, 1900

Are You There?
J. WILLIAMSON
1901–2

Father's Picnic on the Sand
CRICKS AND MARTIN
About 1904

The Gambler's Fate, or The Road to Ruin
. W. PAUL, 1898

Fire!

, WILLIAMSON
901–2

The historical importance of *Fire!*, of which the only known copy is preserved in the National Film Library, warrants inclusion of this unique still despite the extremely poor condition of the print.

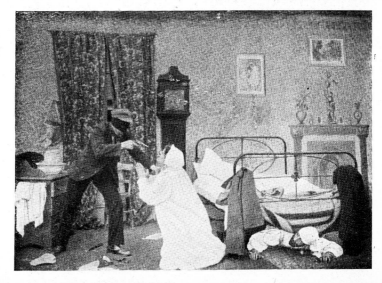

His Brave Defender
, W. PAUL, 1902

28. The Drama of Violence

The Little Witness. G. A. SMITH

The Lover and the Madman. R. W. PAUL, 1905

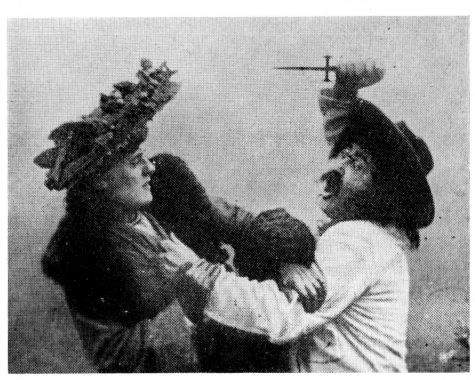

30.
The ? Motorist

R. W. PAUL
1905

31. *The Life of Charles Peace*

WALTER HAGGAR

1905

Rover sets out
to find the
baby
(4 ft.)

runs down the
street
(10 ft.)

round the
corner
(5 ft.)

swims across
the stream
(23 ft.)

inspects the
cottage door
(14 ft.)

and finds the
baby in the
attic
(14 ft.)

He starts the
homeward run
(shot pans
slightly, 5 ft.)

across the
river
(18 ft.)

along the
street
(13 ft.)

and through
the window
(3 ft.)

He pleads
his master
(27 ft.)

and they se
(12 ft.)

across the
(35 ft.)

to the cott
door
(13 ft.)

and claim
the baby
(25 ft.)

to bring h
triumpha
home
(25 ft.)

CECIL HEPWORTH'S *Rescued by Rover* (1905)

The sixteen shots shown above depicted the rescue,
and occupied 300 out of the film's total length of 390 ft.

fortably by the fireside in an arm-chair, and her dreams are shown in this series.

In the first scene she is by the sea shore, and leaving a bathing-tent, she enters the water. A remarkably fine scene shows her adventures at the bottom of the sea, among the fishes and seaweed, at the conclusion of which she rises to the surface, which proves to have frozen. Breaking through the ice she appears in an arctic region, and shivers in her scanty costume. A good fairy appears from the sky, and magically furnishes her with warm furs; then the fairy dissolves into air. The dancer executes a very characteristic dance, and as she is finishing this, flames burst forth, and the view dissolves into a weird fire dance, again changing to the original scene, where the dancer wakes up in a fright, her shoe having caught fire, this causing her to wildly run round the room.

An exceedingly pretty and novel subject, the interest of which is added to by the fact that the scenes are tinted to suit the various surroundings. (Cat. 1906. December 1905.) (180 ft.)

Reversing films had a great vogue:

SHEFFIELD PHOTO COMPANY.   *An Eccentric Burglary*
        THE MOST REMARKABLE FILM EVER PRODUCED

The first scene shows two Burglars climbing over a wall in the Grounds of a Country House. Having gained entrance to the grounds, and finding they cannot enter the house by means of the bottom window, they decide to try the top. They cannot reach stood on one another's shoulders. They plan other means. How is it reached?

These burglars have evidently been trained in a school where acrobatic feats are not unknown, for we see them taking in turn a flying leap from the ground up to the window, unfasten the latch, and enter the room.

The Police now arrive, and also adopt an ingenious method of entering. Having fetched a ladder and placed it against the upper window, THEY SLIDE UP.

In the next scene the Burglars and Police are having an exciting struggle on the roof. They ROLL OVER AND OVER UP THE ROOF, and are then seen CLIMBING DOWN THE HOUSE SIDE HEAD FIRST.

Coming along the road the Burglars see a Cab which they hold up, and drive away with the Police in pursuit.

The scene then changes to another country road, the CAB TRAVELLING BACKWARDS WAY, ditto the Police. The horse comes to a standstill, refuses to move, and SUDDENLY VANISHES. The Burglars take to their heels.

They are next seen rolling up a hill struggling with the Police, who are on the top of them.

Next they come to a long flight of steps leading up to the road. Up the steps the Burglars go, but the Police find an easier method by sliding up the railings. The pursuit is kept up with vigour, Burglars and Police leap over a gate backwards way, and backwards way over a stream, the Burglars turning somersaults. The effect is most curious.

During a desperate struggle the BURGLARS VANISH, only to appear further on the road.

The Police are close on their heels, but the Burglars are now getting exhausted, one is captured, but the other makes a desperate attempt to strangle his pursuer, but the Officer's comrade comes up and deals him a blow with his truncheon. Both the Burglars are then handcuffed and taken into custody. (Cat. 1906. April 1905.) (400 ft.)

On the other hand, the moral element so often present in British cinema of this period guides Haggar in his film described in the Gaumont catalogue of November 1905. *D.T.'s or the Effect of Drink.*

GAUMONT COMPANY. *D.T.'s or the Effect of Drink.* Permission to exhibit in South Wales must be obtained from Messrs Haggar and Sons. A young man, who has just arrived home from his club much the worst[1] for drink is seen entering his bedroom where he at once proceeds to undress, but on taking off his coat and throwing it down it assumes the shape of a dog and walks off; then he fancies that the images on the mantel-shelf have turned into owls, and he gets a broom to clear them off, but on striking them he only succeeds in smashing all the vases. He goes on like this for some time, fancying he sees all manner of things, which on him smashing into only prove to be hat, sticks, chairs, demons and grotesque monsters etc. He at last succeeds in getting into bed, but immediately he lies down the bed shifts its position to the other side of the room, leaving him on the floor; but he quickly picks himself up and gets in once more, but this time the bed turns into a dreadful monster, which takes him round the room on its back, finally disappearing in a cloud of smoke and sending him sky-high. By the time he reaches earth once more and finds that he is all there, he has made a resolution "that he will never get drunk any more."

A capital trick film, splendid subject for showmen. (Cat. November 1905. Not later than August 1905.) (220 ft.)

Hepworth's early comedies made considerable use of trickery; in particular *The Glutton's Nightmare* can be imagined without quoting the detailed synopsis! He made a number of fairly conventional trick films of which *Getting-Up Made Easy* repeats a familiar theme.

[1] Sic.

HEPWORTH MANUFACTURING COMPANY. *Getting-up Made Easy.* What busy man does not know the difficulties attendant upon late rising? This is an amusing film which shows how such troubles are obviated. An old gentleman, upon waking, finds the bedclothes whisked off, and the painful effort of turning out satisfactorily solved. Stepping on to the floor, a portion of his clothes quickly attach themselves and a chair suddenly appears in the centre of the room, upon which the old gentleman seats himself. A wash basin then rolls comically along the floor, and, on being lifted, the water springs from the floor into the basin. Afterwards a looking-glass flies into the old gent.'s hands, and the remainder of his garments having satisfactorily placed themselves, he quits the room well satisfied with the small amount of exertion entailed. (Cat. 1906. January–February 1903.) (100 ft.)

It is to be expected that Hepworth's taste would not long remain satis-fied with these all-too-delightful but all-too-easily-stereotyped subjects. He gives an original twist to the motoring subject:

HEPWORTH MANUFACTURING COMPANY. *How It Feels to be Run Over.* The eccentric artist Wiertz has powerfully depicted the supposed feelings of a decapitated head, but it has remained for the cinematographer to show large audiences what it feels like to be run over. In this very sen-sational picture a pretty country road is seen, and in the distance a dog-cart travelling at a fair speed. The road is narrow, but the cart successfully passes, and as the dust which is raised clears away, a motor car is seen approaching very rapidly indeed. Perhaps it is the dust of the previous vehicle, or perhaps sheer carelessness on the part of the driver, but he does not see the obstruction in the road until it is too late to steer past it. The car comes forward at tremendous speed, and the occupants, realizing the danger, get wildly excited in their efforts to clear the obstruc-tion. The steersman makes one or two frantic swerves, and is seen to apply the brake with all his might, but to no purpose, the car dashes full into the spectator, who sees "stars" as the picture comes to an end. (Cat. 1906. 1900.) (50 ft.)

He made an exceptionally interesting series of scenes from *Alice's Adventures in Wonderland* based on Sir John Tenniel's illustrations "which have been reproduced in animated form with remarkable fidelity". Alice was a wonderful subject for the cinema.

C HEPWORTH. *Alice in Wonderland.* The film is composed of sixteen scenes, dissolving very beautifully from one to another, but preceded, where necessary for the elucidation of the story, by descriptive titles.

Scene 1: Alice falls asleep in a pretty wood. She dreams, and in her dream she sees a White Rabbit, who, after looking at his watch, trots rapidly down a rabbit-hole, and Alice decides to follow him.

Scenes 2 and 3: The Rabbit and Alice disappear into the rabbit-hole and the scene dissolves into the underground passage, along which they both hurry.

Scene 4: Alice now finds herself in the Hall of many Doors. On looking around she discovers on a table a golden key, with which she tries—at first in vain—to open the doors. At last she is successful with one, but discovers that the opening is too small for her to pass through. She now finds a bottle on the table labelled "Drink Me." She tries it and gradually grows smaller and smaller, and, deciding to again try to get through the door, finds she is now unable to reach the table for the key. In despair she weeps, but notices on the floor a cake with "Eat Me" written upon it. She eats, and grows to a huge size, but by fanning herself with the fan left by the Rabbit, she gets smaller again, and this time, having secured the key, succeeds in passing through the little door.

Scene 5: Alice, now very small, has gained access to the Beautiful Garden, and tries to get a big dog to play with her.

Scene 6: In this scene Alice enters the Rabbit's House. When there, she grows large and is almost unable to move, but by fanning herself with the magic fan she very gradually dissolves away.

Scene 7: Shows the exterior of the House, with Alice's huge arm sticking out of the window.

Scene 8: Alice, still fanning herself, gradually appears before the House of the Duchess. The Fish Footman delivers a letter of invitation for the Duchess, to the Frog Footman. Alice, who is an interested spectator of this little episode, decides to go in and see her Grace, and deaf to the Footman's protests enters the house.

Scene 9: Shows Alice entering the Kitchen, where the Duchess is sitting on a stool nursing a Baby; the Cook attending to some soup over the fire. The Cook throws her utensils about in an alarming manner and scatters pepper all over the place, and Alice rescues the Baby and rushes out of the house into the garden, pursued, in Scene 10, by the Mad Cook.

Scene 11: Alice in the garden is seen nursing the Baby, which gradually changes in her arms into a Black Pig.

Scene 12: In this Alice is talking to the Cheshire Cat who directs her to the house of the March Hare.

Scene 13: Represents "The Mad Tea Party." Alice takes tea with the

March Hare, the Mad Hatter, and the Dormouse, but is offended by their behaviour and departs abruptly.

Scene 14: Shows the Royal Procession on its way to the Croquet Ground. The White Rabbit, in full heraldic attire, leads, and is followed by the Royal Gardeners—the 1–10 of Spades. Next come the Courtiers, all decorated with Diamonds, and they are followed by the Clubs, who form a Guard of Honour. The Royal Children (Hearts) come next, and then the Knave, King and Queen of the same suit. The Queen stops, invites Alice to play croquet, and she readily joins them, but they afterwards quarrel.

Scene 15: His Majesty orders "Off with her head," but Alice—having grown to her full size—takes courage and causes great confusion of the Card Courtiers by boxing the ear of the Executioner.

Scene 16: Alice is now seen in the garden waking up, only to discover that it is all a dream.

No pantomime or stage effect is introduced in this film; the whole of the various scenes having been produced in pretty natural surroundings.

Toned and stained in various beautiful colours. (Cat. 1906. Between February and June 1903.) (800 ft.)

(vii) COMEDY

A comedy was the first British "made-up" film, a term used by Hepworth[1] to describe a story film requiring planning and rehearsal. It was produced by R. W. Paul on the roof of the Alhambra in 1896 and was called *The Soldier's Courtship*. It is described by Paul in his catalogue of August 1898 in what was apparently a revised form, as follows:

R. W. PAUL. *Courtship*. The up-to-date edition of the favourite *Soldier's Courtship*, much improved in all respects. The soldier is interrupted in courting a pretty nurse-maid, by an old lady crowding on to the seat and they retaliate by throwing over the seat, which falls on her. Extremely comic, and a fine film. (Cat. 1898.)

It is easy enough to see how the production of simple comic scenes containing their action in a single fifty foot shot developed into what Hepworth calls a "series picture," or a story made-up of a number of single shot incidents grouped together. The beginning of continuity lies

[1] Reference Hepworth's B.K.S. Lecture, p. 10 (February 3, 1936).

in the change from what is in effect a magic-lantern-slide-series technique enlivened by movement in the individual pictures but possessing no organic continuity from one to the other, and the precision of editing which Hepworth's *Rescued by Rover*[1] possesses with the sense of movement emphasized by the linking of the shots which are themselves made more interesting by variety of camera set-up. *Rescued by Rover* shows the beginning of modern film technique with editing playing an important part in the design and movement of the film.

In the comedies and dramas the individual characteristics of the directors become more marked than in any other type of film. Paul's films are interesting both for their lack of subtlety and comparative absence of the more advanced technique to be found in Hepworth's later films made towards 1906. Together with topicals, comedies constitute Paul's main output, yet the comedies are rather comic scenes or comic situations than comic stories. The technique of a comic twist to a story does not appear in his work. He is more fond of knockabout slap-stick or the practical joke. A small proportion of his numerous films deals with the dubious comedy of the domestic dilemma type leading to strife in the home, any example of which seemed to be regarded as exceptionally funny. Though it may be necessary to question Paul's own taste in this matter, there seems little doubt that there was considerable public demand for this type of film. On the other hand, the other chief directors of the period (such as Hepworth, Williamson, Smith, Haggar) do not seem to have made so much game out of marital strife, drunkenness, absence of clothes, physical cruelty and other themes recurrent in Paul's work.

The following are a series of synopses which are interesting from many points of view, as examples of Paul's own work in the period 1898—1906, as examples of public taste in entertainment at the time, and as examples of the stock-in-trade of humour and social behaviour which can be paralleled in the popular literature and music-hall jokes of the first years of the century.

R. W. PAUL. *Come Along, Do!* Outside an exhibition building an old couple from the country take a seat, and begin a meal from their basket, to the amusement of the passers-by. Seeing the people entering the art gallery, the old couple put away their sandwiches and enter. The man

---

[1] See p. 109.

catches sight of a statue of Venus, and examines it with some glee, when he is discovered by the old lady, who leads him away with a most amusing expression. (Listed August 1898. Synopsis 1902 Cat.) (80 ft.)

R. W. PAUL. *Stocks*. The village beadle brings a countryman and woman to the stocks, followed by a crowd of children, milk-maid, etc. The village carpenter is ordered to lock them in, which done, the beadle leaves, and the youngsters pelt the couple with sticks and eggs which smash over them. The parson's wife tries to stop the children, and the beadle at last scatters them. Brilliant, clear and perfectly acted, the expressions being most funny. (Cat. August 1898.) (80 ft.)

R. W. PAUL. *The Tramp and the Turpentine Bottle; or, Greediness Punished*. As the picture opens, a tramp is seen sneaking into a kitchen. Looking around he sees on a shelf a number of bottles—one of these evidently containing beer. He promptly drinks it, but not being satisfied with that, he goes to another bottle of the same shape which is prominently labelled "Turps" on the side he does not see. The extraordinary antics and contortions of his ugly features on getting the full taste of the turpentine produce roars of laughter from the spectators. (Cat. 1902. 1902.) (60 ft.)

R. W. PAUL. *The Curate's Dilemma or the Story of an Ant Hill*. The first scene shows a young curate and some girls going for a treat. They get out of the train and hurry off into the country, where they have games such as skipping, blind-man's buff, etc., after which the curate hands round some refreshment. Being somewhat fatigued after this exercise, he tells them he will go further into the wood to have a rest.

A tramp is next seen taking a seat under a shady tree and shortly after the curate comes along and does the same on the other side. The tramp, finding he has been sitting on an ants' nest, gets up and shakes himself and his rags. The curate falls asleep, but soon awakes with a feeling of discomfort. Finding what he has been lying on he treads on the tiresome insects, shakes his coat and starts off to rejoin the girls.

The party on the railway platform are waiting for the train to take them home. The curate walks about uneasily and on the train arriving, hustles the girls into a carriage and gets into an empty one alone.

Being unable to bear the awful discomfort any longer he pulls down the blinds and hastily removing his trousers, shakes them out of the window, when to his horror they slip from his grasp on to the line. He tries to hide his legs with the tails of his coat but on reaching his destination is obliged to face the position as best he can and rushes off the platform with the now giggling girls. (Cat. 1906. After June 1906.) (290 ft.)

R. W. PAUL. *He Cannot get a word in Edgeways.* Lady is sitting impatiently waiting for her belated husband, who is evidently at the club. He comes at last, and the sight of him causes her to wax furious. She starts nagging and asking questions, he tries to explain, but is not allowed to get a word in. In despair he sits in the arm-chair and starts to read, but she takes the paper away from him and points to the clock. He covers same with his handkerchief, and then tries to put his hat and coat on to go out. She seizes his garments, throws them into a corner and still continues abusing him. In despair he goes to the side-board for whisky and soda. This she grabs at, and throws over him. She is now almost exhausted, when he draws from his pocket a beautiful bracelet, which he gives her. At the sight of the present, the immediate change from the furious woman to the loving wife is very striking, and the picture concludes with a near view of their reconciliation. (Cat. 1906. About June 1906.) (170 ft.)

Williamson's claim to be "funny without vulgarity" which heads his catalogue of September 1899 is just perhaps to the point of over-politeness. He has no films of cruelty, drunkenness or domestic strife. He has some mild knockabout farce among his films:

J. WILLIAMSON. *Washing the Sweep.* Two domestics at wash-tubs in the garden, and hanging clothes out; sweep comes down the path and smudges clothes in passing; "jaw" from the domestics, with some soap-suds added; sweep retaliates with black brush; exciting chase round wash-tubs, sweep trips up, and has his face washed in good style before he can recover. Small terrier assists in a very natural manner. (September 1899.) (60–75 ft.)

He is more interested in romantic farce:

J. WILLIAMSON. *Winning the Gloves.* One of the most popular films. Scene—Garden; Gentleman asleep in hammock chair; lady gathering flowers comes towards gentleman, finding him asleep tickles him, and runs away; comes back, finds him still asleep, kisses him, and runs away again. Gentleman jumps up and rubs his eyes; a friend saunters up, explains that he has lost a pair of gloves, in accordance with ancient custom, pointing towards the fair winner in hiding. Plot to catch the lady: I will pretend to be asleep again. All right, I won't say anything! Waiting, with his eyes closed, in sweet expectation, he feels the breath of the fair one fanning his cheek, jumps up, and puts his arms round—a donkey's neck! (Cat. September 1899.) (65 ft.)

or in straight comedy:

J. WILLIAMSON. *The Fraudulent Beggars*. One labelled deaf and dumb, the other blind, with dog, and reading with fingers from raised type. People passing give coppers; deaf man, forgetting himself, says something to boy passing in, who calls policeman; finds blind man reading comic paper and deaf man laughing at the joke. Free use of policeman's boot; the beggars scramble off. (Cat. September 1899.) (60–75 ft.)

J. WILLIAMSON. *Are You There?* Scene showing two rooms and telephones. Gentleman comes in rings up: "Are you there?" Lady comes to other telephone. "Is that you, Lilian?" "Yes, dear." "Is the old man in?" "No, dear." (Old man listening behind girl). "Can you come round and see me?" "Yes, I'll come round." Hangs up telephone and goes out without seeing old man behind, who catches hold of telephone and listens. Gentleman at other telephone goes on giving girl directions how to come; old man in a towering rage takes the information and uses it to find the next scene, which shows the young gentleman sitting in joyful expectation of his lady love's arrival; he is considerably perturbed when the old man arrives instead and makes effective use of his umbrella. (Cat. September 1902. 1901.) (75 ft.)

Other directors producing typical comedies include Haggar and Clarendon Company, whose films were distributed by Leon Gaumont. The following synopses are taken from the Elge catalogue of November 1905:

W. HAGGAR. *The Rival Painters*. Two rival painters are at work. One is using black paint and the other white, they are having a few words and are apparently very angry with each other. Their anger reaches the climax when their work meets, and blows with the paint brushes ensue; not content with smothering each other with paint, they endeavour to spoil each other's work by slinging paint all over it. A Bobby arrives and endeavours to arrest them, but the result is indescribable confusion and chaotic disorder, in which painters, policemen, paint-pots and brushes, helmets, and truncheons are ingloriously mixed. (Cat. November, 1905. Between May and November, 1905.) (90 ft.)

W. HAGGAR. *Mary is Dry*. The interior of a Public-house bar is shown, and two or three customers are having drinks, and all is peaceful. Mirthful Mary enters, and soon all is chaos, for feeling dry she picks up some of the customers' beer and drinks it off. When they remonstrate with her, however, she picks up a soda-water syphon and thoroughly drenches them. Not content with this, she upsets the tables and smashes the glasses, finally jumping on the counter and wrecking the whole place. (Cat. November 1905. Between May and November 1905.) (94 ft.)

This film was one of the *Mirthful Mary* and *Mary in the Dock* series which Haggar produced.

Father's Hat, or Guy Fawkes Day is one of the first of a long series of comedies made by the Clarendon Film Company and sold through the agency of Gaumont's:

CLARENDON FILMS.   *Father's Hat, or Guy Fawkes Day.*
A TOPICAL COMIC.   NATURAL SCENES.   BRIGHT AND FUNNY.

Scene 1: The back-garden of Mr. Jones's residence. A guy is seated upon a chair placed upon a table in the foreground. The dear children have stolen father's hat, and they come running from the house carrying the topper with care, and scrambling on to the table they arrange the hat on the guy to the best effect. Next they stuff some straw all ready round the feet, and run off to fetch some paraffin to make a good blaze.

Father, however, is on their track and turns up just as the children have gone, and having rescued his hat he suddenly thinks of a plan to catch the children on the hop. First he removes the guy, then slips the mask on to his own face, and jumping up on to the table, he takes the chair and waits.

Scene 2: The dear children are gathered round a huge barrel from which they are drawing a bucket full of paraffin, presently they run off.

Scene 3: Shows father seated as we left him, and the children carrying the bucket come hurrying in—father waits for them to light the straw, not knowing of the paraffin which is behind him. Little Mary does not know that the guy has changed into father, and she throws the paraffin right over him—screams—fire—fire—father in flames—off run the children—father scrambles out of the flames and gives chase. (Cat. October 1904.) (150 ft.)

CLARENDON FILMS.   *The Stolen Purse.*
A CLEVER PLOT.   BEAUTIFUL SCENERY.   EXTREMELY COMIC.

Scene 1: In Regent's Park. Miss Mary Jones is seated comfortably reading the latest fashions when she is suddenly interrupted by a rough-looking man, who asks her the way to Lord's. She politely informs him, and does not notice that while she is speaking he has kicked her purse (which has fallen to the ground) to his friend who is waiting behind the seat. The horrid men are effusive in their thanks, and gaily take themselves off. A fussy old gentleman now makes his appearance, and as he approaches he reads the paper, and not looking at all where he is going, he comes a cropper over the dainty feet of the unfortunate Miss Jones.

It is not until he has taken an apologetic departure that Miss Mary first misses her purse. She calls a constable, and points out the old gentleman; a smart run.

Scene 2: Another part of the Park. The poor old fellow is soon captured; he cannot understand it all. In his struggles he accidentally puts his foot through his hat and is led off vainly expostulating.

Scene 3: An Avenue of Trees. A large crowd are much interested and amused in the struggles of the excited captive, who still has his hat on his foot as he is hurried along.

Scene 4: The Exterior of Miss Jones's House. The fair owner declares that the old gentleman in charge is the man who stole her purse, and he is marched off to the station.

Scene 5: The corner of a most respectable street. A young and smartly-dressed man is approaching, when he is set upon by the two roughs who stole the purse. His cries attract the police, and the roughs are captured.

Scene 6: The Interior of the Police-Station. The roughs are searched, and the purse is found. The old gentleman is brought in, and the purse on the table proves him innocent. He is exasperated to the last degree, but relieves his feelings before going by breaking the seats of the chairs on the heads of the unfortunate officers, whom he leaves vainly struggling for freedom from such painful headgear. (Cat. November 1905. Between August and November 1905.) (315 ft.)

Another firm which specialized in the production of "comics" was Cricks and Sharp:

CRICKS AND SHARP. *The Young Photographer*. Scene: A Surburban Garden. Two young children (boy and girl) are seen entering picture. They find their father's camera and think it would be fine fun to try and use it.

The boy poses his sister in a chair and starts to focus up (here is shown a life-size head of girl which he sees through the camera), but the girl will not sit still and treats the matter as a huge joke. After some very amusing antics she eventually pulls the camera over with her parasol. At this point the father appears on the scene and gives both children a well-merited chastisement. (Cat. undated, apparently 1904.) (70 ft.)

CRICKS AND SHARP. *She* WOULD *Sing*. Scene 1: Drawing Room with ladies and gentlemen in evening dress. Two gentlemen have just finished a duet when a lady (of uncertain age) is asked to oblige. After many excuses she is led to the piano, and, beginning in the wrong key, starts such a burst of melody (?) that the whole company is agitated and makes vain attempts to stop the sound. The lady, however, *would* sing and nothing would stop her, and after many threats she is thrown out of the window.

Scene 2: Exterior of House. The lady is seen falling to the ground, where she continues her song of "Violets." She is, however, chased from the house by the enraged company, who carry various implements—a stout gentleman bringing up the rear with a gun.

Scene 4: The lady comes to a river, followed by the whole company, and as she persists in singing "Violets" she is thrown into the water by two of the gentlemen; and on rising to the surface is *still* singing, when the little fat man comes up with his gun and gives her the *coup de grâce.* (Cat. undated, apparently 1904.) (235 ft.)

The Sheffield Photo Company made its contribution:

SHEFFIELD PHOTO COMPANY. *Bertie's Courtship.* Gerty is enjoying a quiet read in a country lane, when Bertie, a young dandy toff, accosts her, and eventually takes her for a stroll. His enjoyment does not last long, for another male acquaintance comes along, and Bertie gets a good hiding.

In the second scene Bertie and Gerty are sat in a secluded part of the garden, having a quiet spoon, when Gerty's little brother arrives, and upsets the form on which Bertie is sat. In the last scene, Bertie goes to ask Pa's consent, but he returns soon flying down the steps with the indignant Pa after him and moreover Pa's dog takes a dislike to him, and chases him over the garden wall. VERY LAUGHABLE. (Cat. 1906. December 1904.) (95 ft.)

Hepworth, in comparison with Paul, shows a gentler taste, but has much more strength than Williamson. His work, always carefully and even elaborately described in his catalogues, shows the taste of the developing artist who later was to supersede all contemporary workers in film and become the most important producer Britain was to make up to his retirement as a film-maker in the twenties.

His first "made-up" film was a slap-stick called *The Stolen Drink.* He describes it as follows in his 1906 catalogue.

C. HEPWORTH. *The Stolen Drink.* Two ardent supporters of Izaak Walton (and Bacchus) are seated on boxes in a fisherman's punt moored in midstream, and between them is a gallon jar of refreshment. One is more than half asleep when the other steals a pull at the beer-jug. But his comrade wakes in time to catch him at it. Both have presumably arrived at the quarrelsome stage of inebriation, for a fight ensues during which both fishermen fall overboard with the coveted jar. The fight continues in the water until one is exhausted and has to cling to a floating box for support, while the other climbs into the punt again with the treasure, and so gets his drink after all. (Cat. 1906. Before January 1900.) (50 ft.)

Hepworth liked this type of humorous incident and made more films in this style, though not in any great quantity. On the whole, however, knockabout farce plays a small part in his work. Most of his comedies were, to begin with, trick comedies. Later he came to invent and direct the most elaborate straight comedies of the period.

C. HEPWORTH. *The "Lady" Thief and the Baffled Bobbies.* Showing how a quick change burglar eludes the vigilance of the local constables and escapes with the swag under their very noses. First there is a prologue wherein we see a knowing policeman reading the contents of an evening paper, from which he learns of the Great Diamond Robbery and the escape of the lady burglar with the jewels.

Scene 1: Represents a railway station with a train drawing up at the platform. A lady with a portmanteau selects an empty carriage, and the train steams out of the station. As it disappears, two breathless policemen rush after it, but are just too late to board it. So they telegraph on ahead to have the train watched at other stations.

Scene 2: Depicts the interior of the railway carriage occupied by the "lady" thief, who is seen to be divesting herself of her clothes, which she flings out of the window. The disrobing process soon reveals the fact that it is really a man in disguise, and the masculine toilet is hastily completed as the train draws into a station.

In Scene 3 we find two policemen with a newly-received telegram, anxiously awaiting the arrival of the train containing the "lady" of whom they are in search. When the train draws up they do not notice the young man who alights with a portmanteau, and he successfully passes between them while they *cherchent la femme*. Then they proceed to search the train, and quickly discover an article of essential feminine attire, and it dawns upon them—to their intense disgust and dismay—that their quarry has escaped. This is a film of keen and well-sustained comic interest, without "tricks" or "fakes", and absolutely unobjectionable throughout. It is just the sort of thing the public wants. (Cat. 1906. February 1903.) (200 ft.)

C. HEPWORTH. *What the Curate Really did.* This is a film of quite a new character, depicting by means of a graphic vision on the wall the various exaggerations to which a story is subjected in passing from mouth to mouth. The story in its first form is a very simple one: the story of a mild young curate who gives a half-penny to a little baby girl in return for a bouquet of flowers with which she has presented him. Mrs. Jones, who is passing at the time, bows to the curate, but he accidentally neglects to return her salutation. Mrs. Jones, tells the story to Mrs. Brown during tea that afternoon, and by slight exaggeration she makes it appear that the curate has been unnecessarily attentive to a young and pretty school-girl. The story as Mrs. Jones tells it appears in a sort of vision on the back wall of the room. Mrs. Brown is entertained by the little story, and tells it again to Mrs. Robinson, and by this time the story has grown to a con-siderable extent. As it appears above the talker's head, we see the curate paying great attention to a young lady of eighteen or thereabouts, who presents him with a bunch of flowers and receives a small article of jewel-lery in return. Mrs. Robinson is greatly shocked, and when the Bishop comes to tea with her she thinks it necessary to tell him the story, which by this time has grown to really alarming proportions. As the vision of what Mrs. Robinson thinks the curate did rises above their heads, it is easy to understand the horror and indignation manifest on the Bishop's countenance. Off he goes to the curate at once to demand an explanation. The curate is overcome with horror and dismay when he hears the terrible charges laid at his door, but at last a light dawns upon him, and going to the door he calls in his landlady's little baby-girl, and explains to the Bishop that this was the young lady to whom he is said to have paid such disgraceful attention. (Cat. 1906. Between June 1905 and February 1906.) (250 ft.)

(viii) DRAMA

At this early stage differentiation between the various branches of drama (romance, melodrama, drama, tragedy) would be almost impossible. The simplicity of the themes and their treatment is such that the only main distinction lies between the nature of the appeal of the entertainment. If the main object is to cause laughter, then the film can be classed as a comedy, which may range from funny facial expression, to slap-stick and farce, or even sentimental comedy in a few instances. If the main object is to cause an emotional response (sentiment, excitement or the conflict of human relationships) then the film can be classed as drama.

The earliest examples of drama as such appear to be in Paul's catalogues. In his 1898 list he has for example *Deserter* in his "New Series of Specially Fine Comic and Dramatic Films."

R. W. PAUL. *Deserter*. An old woman is seated in a cottage reading; her soldier son enters in civilian clothes, and explains that he has deserted, and is pursued. She hides his uniform, and he conceals himself under the bed. A corporal and two privates come up and look through the window. They demand admittance, and the corporal shows his warrant, detects the uniform, and arrests and handcuffs the deserter, who after a touching farewell with his mother, is led off between the two privates. A perfectly acted and natural scene, which is very pathetic. (Cat. August 1898.) (80 ft.)

Williamson's catalogue of September 1899 contains no dramatic scene. Hepworth's first example seems to have been *The Call to Arms* in March 1902:

C. HEPWORTH. *The "Call to Arms."* How an Englishman responds to his country's need.

Scene 1: Portrays the meeting of a dandy gentleman with two fascinating ladies in a picturesque park. He quickly makes their acquaintance and persuades them to allow him to accompany them on their walk.

In Scene 2 they are found strolling together by an ubiquitous newsboy, who sells the gallant a newspaper containing the country's appeal for volunteers for the front. The leisured swell is fired with patriotic zeal, and hurriedly bidding adieu to his fair friends, he hastens to obey the call, leaving them somewhat dismayed.

Scene 3: Depicts a busy railway station where the sometime dandy—now a khaki-clad soldier—is bidding a last farewell to the many friends who have come to see him off. Then he jumps into the train and is whirled away to active service amid the good wishes of his friends.

Scene 4: Shows him on the veldt, wounded and alone, but still alert and active, lying in a trench with his gun at the "ready." He gets a couple of shots at the enemy, and in Scene 5 we have a glimpse of his home circle anxiously awaiting his return. At the first sound of his approach they rush out to meet him, drag him triumphantly into the room and overwhelm him with joyful congratulations.

This film is a complete little series in itself—a veritable novel in a nutshell. It will form a very welcome change from the hackneyed programme. (Cat 1906. March 1902.) (150 ft.)

Paul in his catalogue of 1902 was still producing sentimental or dramatic *scenes* alongside more advanced story films. Both have remarkable period value as regards the attitude to sentiment and emotional values.

R. W. PAUL. *Sentimental Song with Animated Illustrations "Ora Pro Nobis"; or The Poor Orphan's Last Prayer.* As the picture opens, the villagers are entering the porch of their picturesque old church, while a snow-storm rages and the lights of the church stream out over the snow-clad gravestones. On one of these a young girl dressed in rags is resting. A lady, passing into the church, stops and speaks to the waif and gives her a copper. The child wearily drags herself to the church door and listens to the music, her face beaming with delight. Weakened by exposure, she totters towards a cross on one of the graves, at which she prays, and falls exhausted on the snow. An angel descends, and carries her spirit upwards. The sexton finding her dead, obtains assistance and carries her off. This scene illustrates the well-known song of the same name, and is highly suitable for use in connection with it or otherwise at church entertainments, being beautifully executed. Price 75s. (100 ft.)

Music published by Orsborn and Company, 63 Berners Street, W. Set of Slides for use with song, completing the incidents, Plain, 12s.; Coloured, 24s. (Cat. 1902. About June 1902.)

R. W. PAUL. *Plucked from the Burning.* A very realistic and thrilling picture of the interior of a house on fire; a mother and child are awakened by the smoke, and the distracted parent picks up the baby and rushes to the door, only to be beaten back by flames. A fireman, climbing up to the window, carries away the child, but the mother faints and falls. The fireman returns and is unable to get the woman through the window, but hastily chopping out the sash he carries her out just as, amid clouds of smoke, the ceiling falls. (Cat. 1902. Probably 1898.) (100 ft.)

R. W. PAUL. *The Gambler's Fate, or The Road to Ruin.* Scene 1: In the drawing-room of a fashionable gambling house, a dupe is playing nap with two sharpers. Having lost, and being pressed by an adventuress to play again, he signs an I.O.U., and another game is played with the same result. He detects one of the sharpers cheating, and tries to recover the paper, but is forestalled by the lady, who waves it in his face. Becoming desperate, he fires on the cheat, and, leaving him mortally wounded escapes in the confusion.

Scene 2: The murderer, having escaped to his home, is at the table with his wife, who vainly offers him food. He cannot eat; and when his child is brought in to say "goodnight," he is in despair. The servant runs in, followed by a sergeant and policeman bearing a warrant for his arrest. His wife begs him to tell her what it means, but he hangs his head, and will not speak. He is searched, the revolver is taken from him, and after being handcuffed he is taken from his home, bidding a touching farewell.

96

A most impressive film, giving a strong moral lesson. (Cat. 1902.) 200 ft.)

R. W. PAUL. *The Artist and Flower Girl.* On a cold winter's night the struggling artist hears a noise outside the studio, and finds that a flower girl has fainted in the snow. He brings her in, covered with snow, and revives her with a cordial. Hearing some convivial friends coming, he hides her behind a screen, but they find her hat upon the floor. The artist persuades them to leave. The weary artist bows his head on his hands, and the girl, having heard the remarks of his friends, silently leaves him her stock, and wiping away a tear of gratitude, creeps off unobserved. (Cat. 1902. Probably 1898.) (80 ft.)

Williamson in his catalogue of September 1902 has an advanced dramatic story called *The Soldier's Return.*

J. WILLIAMSON. *The Soldier's Return.* A bit of real life. There is no suggestion of acting in the picture, and the setting is perfectly natural. In four scenes.

Scene one shows a portion of a row of poor cottages—one occupied, another empty. Soldier walks in with his kit bag on his shoulder, tries the door, peeps in the window, looks up to the top window—the cottage is evidently deserted; a woman comes out of the next cottage and says something to him—no doubt with reference to the late occupant, which appears to upset the soldier a good deal; a blacksmith walks up, claims acquaintance, and is warmly greeted; the soldier hands his bag to the woman next door to look after, and walks away.

Next scene shows the outside of workhouse; soldier enters, presents a paper to the gate porter, who looks at it and points out the direction in which he is to go.

The next scene shows the door of the women's ward, the soldier walks in, knocks at the door, which is opened by a nurse who looks at his paper and goes in again, soldier waiting outside: after a short interval an old lady in workhouse garb appears, evidently the mother of the soldier, as they warmly embrace—a pathetic picture, true to life. The soldier indicates that he has come to fetch her home, and motions to her to go and change her clothes; he helps her up the steps, and walks to and from while the old lady is dressing. After a short time she comes out again dressed in her own clothes—the soldier takes her arm and walks away with her; they only get a few steps, however, before they are called back by the other old inmates, who have followed the old lady, to shake hands, congratulate her and wish her good-bye.

Another short scene shows them walking out of the gate.

The last scene shows the outside of the cottage again—but what a change! The windows cleaned, clean curtains up, flowers in the window, a bird in a cage hanging up by the door; the old woman sitting by the door sewing, while her son in his shirt sleeves is planting some flowers in the little slip of garden in front—he stops to light his pipe, and asks if that will do; the old lady nods approval, and he resumes his work. He looks up again later and says something to her, and then goes into the cottage and brings out a cup of tea and hands it to his mother; the picture closes just as she is drinking the tea. (Cat. September 1902. May–June 1902.) (185 ft.)

Another elaborate story film by Williamson is *Fire*: described by him as "undoubtedly the most sensational fire scene which has yet been kinematographed, and never fails to arouse the utmost enthusiasm. To enhance the effect, portions of the film are stained red."

J. WILLIAMSON. *Fire!* First Scene: Policeman on his beat in the early morning finds an unoccupied portion of a building well alight with window burnt out, while the inmates of the adjoining part are apparently asleep and unconscious of their danger. He endeavours to arouse them, and tries to open door, blows his whistle to call assistance and rushes off to call the fire engine and escape.

Second Scene: Outside the fire station; policeman rushes in, shakes the door and rings the bell; fireman opens door, policeman excitedly gives particulars of fire, other firemen hurry forward, dressing as they go and quickly rush off with small fire escape. In an incredibly short time a horse is fixed to another escape, and two horses into a manual engine, and the whole gallop off.

Third Scene: Shows horsed fire escape and engine coming full gallop past the camera.

Fourth Scene: Interior of bedroom full of smoke; man in bed just rousing; discovering room full of smoke he jumps out of bed and throws contents of water jug over the fire, then rushes to the door and opens it, but finds his passage blocked by flame and smoke; he then goes towards the window, but just at that moment the curtains set alight, and overcome by smoke and heat he buries his head in the bedclothes. The window curtains and blind now burnt away disclose a fireman outside with hatchet breaking in the window; he comes in with his hose and quickly extinguishes the fire; he then goes to the relief of the man now helpless on the bed, and puts him across his shoulder, and carries him to the window.

Fifth Scene: Shows the outside of the window; fireman with rescued man across his shoulders comes down escape; another fireman runs up and fetches down the hose, throwing out some bedclothes to put round the rescued man; the latter recovering his senses recollects that there are others in the burning building. One fireman, laying a wet cloth over his mouth, breaks into a French window, while others hurry away with the escape to another part of the building. Fireman re-appears through the smoke with a child in his arms, the previously rescued man clutching the child from him hurries away with her, overjoyed at her rescue. Meanwhile the captain has directed another party of firemen to prepare to rescue another inmate, who appears at the window in an exhausted condition; the fire escape being occupied elsewhere, the jumping sheet is brought into requisition, and the man jumps into it and is carried away by the firemen. (Cat. September 1902. 1901–2.) (280 ft.)

Hepworth's lists contain many examples of dramas and thrillers made between 1902–6. An elaborate one is *A Den of Thieves*

C. HEPWORTH. *A Den of Thieves.* A stirring and exciting picture giving the story of a crime from its conception to the arrest of the criminals.

Scene 1: Exterior of Mr. William Johnson's House in the Suburbs. Postman delivers a registered letter, which is signed for by the housemaid.

Scene 2: Interior of Kitchen. Housemaid opens letter by steaming it over a kettle, finds that it contains a cheque for a large amount, and seals it up again.

Scene 3: The Breakfast Room. Mr. and Mrs. Johnson at breakfast. The housemaid brings in the letter and overhears Mr. Johnson's intention of cashing the cheque at once.

Scene 4: Interior of Robber's Den. Two typical burglars and a woman confederate are sitting round a table playing cards, and smoking and drinking. Mr. Johnson's housemaid gives the recognized signal and is admitted. She tells her confederates about the cheque, and the robbers together conceive a plan of attack.

Scene 5: Exterior of the House. The robber, disguised as a clergyman, is lurking about waiting for Mr. Johnson to leave. When he does so, he is followed by the robber and the woman.

Scene 6: At the Bank. Mr. Johnson enters and receives cash for his cheque, while the thieves wait outside for him. He gets into an omnibus, and the man and woman jump in beside him.

Scene 7: At the Railway Station. Mr. Johnson enters a first-class carriage, and the clergyman and woman seat themselves one on either side of him.

Scene 8: The train leaves the Station and enters a long tunnel.

Scene 9: Interior of the Railway Carriage. The woman engages Mr. Johnson's attention, while the robber attacks him from behind, and, after a determined struggle, throws him to the ground and takes the money from him. The robber jumps out of the train, but the woman is caught and held tightly by the victim.

Scene 10: At the Next Station. Mr. Johnson calls the police and gives the woman in charge, and tells them of the robbery which has been committed.

Scene 11: Exterior of the House. Mr. Johnson with the two policemen and the woman prisoner, arrive and take the housemaid by surprise. The woman denounces the girl as an accomplice and informant, and she falling on her knees, promises to confess everything and to lead the police to the robbers' den.

Scene 12: Interior of Robbers' Den. The thief has just arrived with the money, which he and his confederate hide in a hole in the floor. Suddenly they hear alarming sounds outside, and they bolt the door tightly and barricade it by heaping boxes and chairs and everything they can find against it. But the police outside smash the door in, and bursting through, cover the men with revolvers. There is a terrific struggle, in which one robber is knocked senseless, and the other man, held at bay by the revolver pointed at his head, is gradually forced to reveal the place where the money is hidden. The gold is taken from the hole in the floor and returned to its owner, and the thieves and their accomplices are taken into custody. (Cat. 1906. Between June 1904 and February 1905.) (425 ft.)

To show how the film in Britain was growing in length and complexity the full synopsis of *Falsely Accused* is quoted. This film is almost one reel long (850 ft.; running time 14 minutes approximately), and had thus reached the stage of development immediately preceding the feature film, which was to develop in the principal film producing countries in the next few years (1906–14).

C. HEPWORTH. *Falsely Accused.* A very powerful and dramatic film, telling vividly and lucidly a strong story of the highest interest, sustained throughout.

Scene 1: Interior of an Office in the City. Two or three clerks are larking together, when the Principal arrives, and serious work commences for the day. On opening his letters the Principal finds a number of bank notes, and hands them to one of the clerks, to place them immediately in the safe. The clerks turns over and checks the notes. As he does so the numbers are revealed to the audience by means of a short telescopic view. A fellow-clerk of forbidding aspect, looks over his shoulders meanwhile and observes the value of the notes. They are placed in the safe, but the clerk is called away for a moment before he has time to lock it. The sinister-looking man withdraws the key, and makes an impression on a piece of soap before he replaces it; the first clerk then locks the safe and hands the key back to his employer.

Scene 2: Midnight. The office is in inky darkness, when the wicked-looking clerk enters with a lantern and prowls along until he comes to the safe. He takes from his pocket the false key which he has made from his soap impression, and fitting it in the lock, he is able to obtain the coveted notes. He closes and re-locks the safe, and then the full extent of his villainy becomes apparent. Making his way to his fellow-clerk's desk at the other side of the room, he places two of the notes and the impression of the key in the drawer, and leaving this terribly incriminating evidence behind him makes his way cautiously to the door.

Scene 3: The same office next morning. On his arrival the Principal himself goes to the safe and at once misses the stolen notes. In the midst of the scene of consternation which follows, the villain steps forward and suggests that the last man to handle the notes should really know more about them than he seems to, and advises that his desk be searched. After some natural hesitation this is done, and the incriminating evidence brought to light. (Again the audience sees clearly in a telescopic view the unmistakable impression of a key in a bit of soap.) The master and the fellow-clerks see this, and the evidence appears overwhelming, but the unhappy man protests his innocence so fervently that for a moment he is believed, and he leaves the office before anyone thinks of stopping him.

Scene 4: The Hero's Home. The luckless man arrives unexpectedly, and his wife greets him with delight until he tells her of the terrible accusation which has been brought against him. While he is in the middle of the recital the police arrive, and before his wife's eyes he is taken captive and dragged away to await his trial.

Scene 5: The Quarries. Evidently he has failed to establish his innocence before a jury of his fellow-men. Here he is in convict garb, working steadily with pick-axe, among men of a ruder build. But his fellow-workers are sympathetic, and knowing his story, have agreed to help him in his plot to escape. While the warder's back is turned for a moment, engaged in quelling an imaginary dispute between other convicts, the hero makes a wild dash for liberty. The warder shoots at him but misses, and then, calling another warder, starts off in pursuit.

Scene 6: The Escaped Convict. By a clever ruse the hero puts his pursuers off the scent for a moment and increases the distance between them.

Scene 7: At Bay. The convict climbs over the Vicarage wall and makes his way into the garden.

Scene 8. In the Vicarage Garden. The convict pushes his way cautiously through the bushes, and then makes a dash through the opening across the lawn and through the French windows into the Vicar's study.

Scene 9: The Vicar's Study. The Vicar is seated at his table quietly writing when he becomes aware of the presence of a convict. Seizing the revolver which lies always ready at hand—for an escaped convict is to be dreaded so near to the prison—he presents it full at the hunted man. The hero falls upon one knee, and bares his breast for the shot, for all seems lost. The Vicar, impressed with the man's face, asks for his story, which the hero gives in as few words as possible. Then the Vicar, believing in his innocence, decides to help him, and, just in time, he thrusts him into an inner room to change his costume. Meanwhile the warders arrive, and, with many apologies, assert that it is their duty to search the house, for they have been told that the convict is hiding there. The Vicar holds them in conversation for a short time, and while they are talking the convict, now a very presentable-looking curate, strolls into the room, and seats himself at the table, and the warders, suspecting nothing, go off to search the house. Meanwhile their quarry escapes.

Scene 10: Homeward Bound. The young man is running across the lawn when the Vicar calls him back, and pointing out that he is absolutely penniless and therefore helpless, lends him sufficient money to carry him back to his home.

Scene 11: The Gambling Den. We now leave the hero for a while and follow the fortunes of the heartless man who has caused all the trouble: he is the possessor of the stolen notes, but for the present he does not dare to use them. Meanwhile his gambling instincts are as rife as ever, and he is seen in this picture to be making his way to a small gambling den in the neighbourhood of Soho. But the police have spotted the place, and after his entry have quietly drawn a cordon around it.

Scene 12: The Raid. In the interior of the gambling den the play is evidently going against the "toff"; constantly he stakes and loses, and then swears he will play no more. His companions jeer at him: the "gentleman" is broke at last, and it is evident they have no love for him. Maddened by their taunts, however, he draws the stolen notes from his pocket, and, pushing them on the table, challenges the players to win them from him. But at that moment the cry of "Police!" goes round, and all is blank confusion and dismay. The villain, overcome with the strangeness of it all, seizes the notes again, and is caught by the police with them in his hand. One of the policemen had given evidence at the trial of the innocent clerk, and the facts of that case were still fresh in his memory. As soon as he sees the notes he is caught by the numbers of them and compares then with his pocket-book. Then he indeed has a clue, and the villain, feeling that the toils are closing around him, makes one desperate dash for liberty, but is stopped and carried off by his captors.

Scene 13: The Hero's Home-coming. The hero, still in his curate's clothes rushes home and comforts his disconsolate wife, but their joy is short-lived, for the tramp of a policeman is heard on the stair. The "curate" is pushed into an inner room, and his wife stands outside the door when the policeman enters. He keeps her in suspense for a moment or two, and then reveals the fact that he is the bearer of a free pardon to her husband. The wife, now all jubilant, rushes to the door and calls her husband in. He is chaffed a little by the friendly policeman on account of his strange clothes; but, caring nothing for that, the happy couple think only of their reunion.

Scene 14: Justice. In the last scene we have a glimpse of the wicked thief in convict clothes behind his prison bars. He is mad with rage and passion and tears wildly at the irons—but for him there is no escape. (Cat. 1906. Between February and June 1905.) (850 ft.)

The action in such a film as this has reached a stage of complexity that only requires the addition of properly developed characterization to produce the modern feature film. Like all its contemporaries, it relies solely on narrative-action to keep its interest alive. With the Sheffield Photo Company's famous *Life of Charles Peace*, it seems to have been one of the longest films produced in the first ten years of the British cinema. The Sheffield Photo Company, probably more than any other British company, was world-famous for its long and ambitious filmed dramas (distributed by the Charles Urban Trading Company), many of which contained the well-known "chase" and were, in fact, short adventure stories. *The Daring Daylight Burglary* of early 1903 was the Sheffield Photo Company's first effort in this direction, followed later in the year by *Robbery of the Mail Coach*. The most ambitious example, *The Life of Charles Peace*, was made a couple of years later, in November 1905.[1]

CHARLES URBAN TRADING COMPANY. *A Daring Daylight Burglary.*
The opening scene shows the garden of a gentleman's country house. The burglar enters the yard by scaling the wall, and after looking round,

---

[1] The Sheffield Photo Company's version of the *Life of Charles Peace*, a synopsis of which is reproduced here, was actually no more advanced than that of the lesser-known producer Walter Haggar, whose production in fact preceded the other by some months. It is Haggar's film, and not the S.P.C.'s as formerly supposed, which is preserved in the National Film Library.

cautiously breaks open the window and enters the house. Meanwhile, a boy has observed the burglar at his task from the top of a wall, and the scene then changes to the village police-station, showing the boy running in and informing the police. The policemen enter the yard by the wall, one goes inside the house while the other keeps watch. The scene then changes to the house-top where a desperate struggle ensues between the policeman and burglar in which the former is *thrown from the roof* to the road below.

The scene next changes to the road where the body of the policeman is lying. His comrade summons the Ambulance which arrives and conveys the body to the mortuary.

Meanwhile, two policemen take up the chase along a country road, where another desperate struggle takes place. The burglar throws his assailant to the ground and escapes over the wall, hotly pursued by another policeman.

The next scenes depict the exciting chase down the cliff, over the stepping stones of the river.

The scene again changes to a country railway station showing the train. Just as the train moves off, the burglar rushes across the platform and enters a compartment. The policeman is seen hurrying after his quarry, but too late. The last picture shows another railway station, some miles away, to which the police have telegraphed, and just as the burglar alights from the train he is promptly captured by a policeman, but only after a terrible struggle in which the burglar is thrown to the ground, and with the assistance of porters he is eventually handcuffed and marched off, forming a splendid and rousing finish to one of the most sensational pictures ever cinematographed. *Creates unbounded applause and enthusiasm.* (Cat. November 1903. Early 1903.) (275 ft.)

CHARLES URBAN TRADING COMPANY. *Robbery of the Mail Coach.* The film commences showing the exterior of a roadside Inn, where the landlord and a country yokel are seated, smoking and drinking, when they catch sight of the coach. The coach pulls up, and passengers alight and partake of refreshments. The coach drives off and scene changes to a cross road. The coach is seen approaching. Suddenly two highwaymen appear on the scene, and calling to the passengers "Hands up," shoot both the driver and guard. They proceed to relieve the passengers of their valuables, one of the lady passengers meanwhile having fainted, and another stubbornly resisting her persecutors. Having attained their object, they mount their steeds, raise their hats, and ride away. Shortly after two Kingsmen ride up, evidently seeking information as to the whereabouts of the highwaymen, and having acquired same, ride away in pursuit.

The next scene shows the wayside Inn to which the highwaymen ride up and dismount and enter for refreshments. Whilst inside the Kingsmen arrive, and having asked and obtained information of the landlord, enter the Inn. Meanwhile the highwaymen have seen their approach, and the scene changes to the back of the Inn, where the highwaymen are seen to throw a rope from an upper window and escape by this means. The Kingsmen perceiving the rope at the window, follow.

The scene again changes to a pretty river scene into which the highwaymen leap in their endeavour to escape. In the rush across the stream one of them shoots at their pursuers but without effect.

The film is now reaching an exciting stage and two changes of scene take place, in which the pursuit is hotly continued, many pistol shots being exchanged.

Next is seen a clump of trees, out of which pursuers and pursued emerge. A desperate struggle takes place, in which the Kingsmen are thrown to the ground. The highwaymen manage to escape but lose their pistols in the encounter.

The next and last scene showing a tree into which the highwaymen climb in a vain endeavour to elude their pursuers. They are discovered in the act by the Kingsmen who raise their pistols and shoot. Both highwaymen are seen to fall violently from the tree to the ground. Whilst the Kingsmen are attending to one, the other with difficulty endeavours to get away but is promptly shot in the attempt, making a thrilling finish to an exciting and novel subject.

A film that is full of exciting incidents and of a unique and novel character. All the dresses in this picture are the style of 100 years ago. All the scenes are well-chosen, including the Inn, which was a popular calling place in the old coaching days of that period. (Cat. November 1903. After September 1903.) (375 ft.)

SHEFFIELD PHOTO COMPANY.

The Life of Charles Peace, the Notorious Burglar.

THE SCENES OF THESE INCIDENTS WHICH OCCURRED AT NIGHT ARE ARTISTICALLY PRINTED BLUE.

A Film of intense interest and excitement. Every attempt has been made to make this film as exact in detail as possible. The Banner Cross Murder, *taken on the actual spot*; the Sensational Leap from the Train, *taken on the actual spot*.

Scene 1: The opening Scene shows the Prince of Burglars at work as a Picture Framer.

Scene 2: Whilst Peace was living in Darnall, a suburb of Sheffield, he became on very friendly terms with a neighbour, Mr. Dyson, and his wife, and was in the habit of calling and entertaining them with his violin, playing on which he was very clever. Unfortunately he became too fond of Mrs. Dyson, and on one occasion Mr. Dyson caught him embracing his wife. Enraged at this, he turned Peace out of his house. These incidents are depicted in this scene.

Scene 3: Shows Dyson throwing a note into Peace's garden, which forbids his unwelcome intrusions into his family. Peace is enraged, and from this moment he evidently formed an intense hatred of Mr. Dyson.

Scene 4: *The Murder at Banner Cross.* Peace conceals himself in Dyson's garden at night. Mrs. Dyson crosses the garden, but Peace springs out of his hiding place and annoys her. Mr. Dyson hearing a noise comes out of his house, and Peace runs away towards the street, Dyson following. Peace turns round and fires at Dyson, and at the second shot he falls mortally wounded. Peace makes off over the fields.

Scene 5: Peace commits a burglary at Manchester and is captured by the Police.

Scene 6: Peace approaches a house at night, carrying his Violin Case, in which he usually carried a Rope Ladder to enable him to scale high walls, etc. He throws the ladder on to the wall and climbs over.

Scene 7: The Interior of the House. After fastening up the door, he ransacks the Safe of its silver and jewellery.

Scene 8: Whilst hiding his spoil in a field he is watched and captured after a desperate struggle.

Scene 9: *How Peace deceived the Police.* After the last incident, Peace was convicted and sentenced to a long term of imprisonment. This scene illustrates the cleverness of the man in disguising himself. The police being on his track he finds a quiet spot, and taking from his Violin Case a change of clothes and make-up, he so completely disguises himself as to be able to put the police off the scent when they meet him.

Scene 10: A desperate encounter with the Police.

Scene 11: Peace commits a Burglary at Blackheath; the Attempted Murder of P.C. Robinson; and Final Capture. Peace is here shown breaking into a house at Blackheath. Two Policemen on their night beat notice a light in an upper window, and being suspicious, keep watch. P.C. Robinson sees Peace leaving the house. Peace sees him, and fires several shots, the last hitting the constable in the arm. The plucky constable however sticks to his opponent, and is successful in holding him until the arrival of his comrades, when he is handcuffed and taken to the lock-up.

Scene 12: *The Sensational Leap from the Train.* When Peace was brought from London to Sheffield for trial he conceived the idea of escaping from the train by jumping through the window. In this scene, just as the train is passing between Kiveton Park and Shireoaks, Peace is seen to suddenly make a leap through the carriage window, but one of the warders in charge catches hold of his foot, but Peace manages to kick off his shoe and falls on the line. Unfortunately for himself he is injured by the force of the fall, and is unable to crawl into the wood (which was his intention) before the train had been stopped, and he is in the hands of the warders, who carry him away and place him in the guard's van.

This was the last incident in Peace's criminal career before his Trial and Execution at Armley Goal, near Leeds. It has been decided NOT to reproduce the Execution scene, as we believe it is too ghastly and repulsive. All the Scenes are Titled. (Cat. 1906. November 1905.) (870 ft.)

Examples of the adventure story are found in the work of other producers:

W. HAGGAR. *Salmon Poachers: A Midnight Melee.* The scene opens in a picturesque spot, where we see the salmon-poachers busy at work with the nets; but the authorities getting wind of their depredations arrive on the scene in a boat. The poachers, hastily gathering up their catch of eight or ten fine fish, make off. They are met, however, as they climb up the bank by two policemen, but after a struggle the policemen are flung into the river. They escape; but the minions of the law are upon their track and soon come upon them. A realistic fight takes place and the poachers make off again, but leaving their fish behind them, which a corpulent policeman promptly gathers up and takes away. The chase continues and they are eventually run to earth, and after some difficulty placed in a boat to be taken to the lock-up. They are not at the end of their resources, however, and make another bold bid for freedom while in the boat, and succeed in pitching their captors into the water, beating them off with the oars. They finally escape in the boat, leaving their discomforted pursuers struggling in the water.

Magnificent quality throughout, and beautifully tinted. This is the most realistic "moonlight effect" picture we have ever issued. (Cat. November 1905. Between August and November 1905.) (274 ft.)

CLARENDON COMPANY. *The Stolen Bride.* An excellent story. Holds an audience. Magnificent finish.

Mr. Von Potstousen has decided to force his daughter to marry a man of his own selection whether she likes it or not. She does not like it, and when she finds that tearful expostulation is of no use she writes to her lover Jack Strongly, telling him that unless he rescues her on the way to the church she will unavoidably be wedded on the morrow. Jack is a man of resource, and instantly hits on a plan of campaign. He engages a motor boat and waits by a ford in the river where the carriages are bound to cross on their way to the church. The bride's carriage duly arrives, and Jack dashes into the water, throws open the door, and carries off the bride in triumph, leaving Mr. Potstousen speechless with surprise. He places his sweetheart gently in the launch and away they go. Arrived on the opposite shore they hurry up to the church. Meanwhile the father has secured a boat and is hot in pursuit, and just when the young couple are overcoming the objections of the parson, father arrives on the scene. Jack is frustrated and sent off, while Edna is marched away by her father and the clergyman.

Then comes the surprise—Jack is not done yet. Hurrying down to the river he bores a large hole in the bottom of Mr. P.'s boat, then boarding his own vessel he anxiously awaits the result. Presently Von. P. and his daughter start off on their return journey in the deepest dudgeon. Their temper, howevers, suffers a sudden change when they discover that the boat is leaking and must soon sink. At this point Jack arrives on the scene in his motor boat, and dashing up at full speed rescues the girl of his heart just in time to save her from a ducking. Jack now holds the strong position, and refuses to rescue father till he agrees to his terms. Slowly the boat is sinking, and Mr. Von P. is getting more desperate every minute. Not till the very last does he give in, when, having been ignominiously hauled from the water up-side-down, he shows gratitude to his future son-in-law by giving him his blessing. (Cat. October 1906.) (650 ft.)

The most famous story film of the period is Cecil Hepworth's *Rescued by Rover*. Made in 1905, it featured his wife and daughter (a baby), his dog Rover and two hired actors. The scenario was written by Mrs. Hepworth, and the total cost of production was £7 13s. 9d. 395 prints were sold. In the end Hepworth re-made the film twice, producing therefore three versions because he twice wore out his negative to meet the demand for positive prints selling at £10 12s. 6d. each. (The film ran 425 ft. or about seven minutes). Although it was by no means the longest film of its period (*Falsely Accused* was exactly twice as long) this film had a genuine sense of continuity, revealing therefore an advanced form of film technique such as Griffith was to work out in his films. It employs low-camera-angle to match the height of the dog as it runs down the street. Above all it moves rapidly from scene to scene, employs a variety of indoor and outdoor settings, and the shots of the dog running, swimming, jumping, have a forward drive of movement which is carefully matched by the cutting of the film. We quote it therefore in conclusion as a favourable example of British film technique in narrative for the period ending 1906.

C. HEPWORTH. *Rescued by Rover*. An altogether charming subject, absolutely new in conception and realization.

In a luxurious house a little baby, an only child, is lying peacefully asleep, guarded by a faithful Collie dog three times her size. The dog appears to be fully sensible to his privilege as guardian of his master's choicest treasure, and the child seems safe enough in his care. But in the afternoon the baby is taken out by her nurse, and that nurse is interested in a young soldier who meets her by accident in the park every afternoon. While the nursemaid is pushing the perambulator along and wondering when Alphonso will appear, a wicked-looking beggar woman asks for alms, but receives only a haughty refusal. A little further on the nurse-maid meets Alphonso and turns her back on her sleeping charge, while she lights his cigarette. During this absorbing process, the gipsy woman glides up behind, steals the sleeping baby from the perambulator, and makes off as quickly as she can.

In the next scene the mother of the child is doing some fancy-work, when the remorse-stricken nurse bursts into the room and confesses to the loss of the child. Overcome with grief, the poor mother tries to elicit the tragic story from the hysterical girl, and the dog, who is listening intently, licks her face for a moment by way of comforting her, and then starts off with a look of set intention in his faithful eyes. No door is open, so he jumps out of the window, rushing quickly down the street, round several corners, but is baffled for the moment when he comes to a stream, and finds no means of crossing it. Sure he is on the right track, however, he plunges in and swims across, and then makes his way straight to a slum where there is a row of tiny and forbidding-looking houses. He goes systematically along the row, and tries every door, one after the other, always unerringly following the scent, until he comes to the right one, and pushing the door open, runs straight in.

The scene changes to the interior of a filthy attic. The old woman has just arrived with the child, and she proceeds to divest it of its rich clothing. Then leaving the almost naked baby on a heap of rags, she retires to a corner and gloats greedily over the pretty clothing with which the loving mother has decked her baby but a few hours before. Then the dog breaks into the room and runs fondly to the child, whom he caresses in doggy fashion, until the old woman, with shouts and drunken curses, chases him from the garret. Out he runs as quickly as he can, out from the dirty slum into the wider streets, back to the river, which he quickly swims again, back through the various streets he had before traversed, until he arrives at his master's house, jumps in at the window and makes his way to the study, and runs to his master, who is trying in vain to think of a way to recover his darling child. The dog jumps up to him, pushes his nose into his hand, and does everything in his power to attract attention. At first the bereaved father pushes him away, but the dog grows so insistent, runs barking to the door and back with such evident meaning that at last the father decides to follow. Then the faithful dog pushes open the door, and starts to lead his master to the gipsy's garret, constantly looking back to see that he is being followed. He runs along the various streets until he reaches the bank of the river, and plunges in without hesitation. The father, impressed now with the reality of the chase, jumps in a boat and follows. He is led by the faithful dog right through the slum to the very house, and right up into the room where the child lies on a heap of rags. Quickly and fondly the poor father seizes his little daughter, and without stopping to pay much attention to the drunken old woman, who tries to bar his way, he rushes home again, and places the baby in its mother's arms, while the dog, almost dancing for joy, impartially licks the faces of master and mistress and little playmate. (Cat. 1906. Late 1905.) (425 ft.)

APPENDICES

First Recorded or Claimed Demonstrations and Public Performances in Great Britain of Motion Pictures Projected on to a Screen.

		1899	Louis Augustin Le Prince of Leeds said to have projected motion pictures on to the wall of his workshop.
Feb.	25	1890	Friese-Greene said to have demonstrated projection before members of the Bath Photographic Society.[1]
Feb.		1895	R. W. Paul said to have succeeded in projecting motion pictures in his London workshop at Hatton Garden.
Jan.	14	1896	Birt Acres demonstrated the projection of motion pictures before members of the Royal Photographic Society.
Jan.	15	1896	Birt Acres demonstrated the projection of motion pictures before members of the Photographic Club.
Feb.	20	1896	M. Trewey demonstrated the Cinematograph of the French Lumière brothers at the Regent Polytechnic, London. (The public paid admission fee—the beginnings of commercial cinema.)
Feb.	20	1896	R. W. Paul demonstrated his Theatrograph at the Finsbury Technical College.
March 8		1896	R. W. Paul demonstrated his machine at the Royal Institute.
March 9		1896	The Lumière machine moved to the Empire, London. (Commercial.)
March		1896	R. W. Paul's machine was shown at Olympia. (Commercial).
March		1896	Birt Acres' machine was shown in Piccadilly. (Commercial).
March 25		1896	R. W. Paul's machine moved to the Alhambra, London. (Commercial.)

[1] Accounts in the *Amateur Photographer*, March 7, 1890 and the *Photographic News*, March 7, 1890, show that this was not in fact a true demonstration.

Memoirs of Cinema Pioneers

Reminiscences from the unpublished Notebooks of James Williamson, 1926.[1]

Thirty years ago the Kinematograph was certainly an infant. No one knowing the manner of its inception at that day would have ventured a prediction as to what the infant would become; whether it would pass through progressive stages to the successful and revered J.P., or by successive debasements to the abject beggar of Cassell's advertisement, so familiar in those days. For this reason perhaps people of money and influence who could have put the business quickly on a good footing were shy and adopted a policy of "wait and see."

A man who to-day wishes to join the Kinematograph business in any productive department has only to spend money to get everything necessary including skilled workers. In 1896 one could not buy anything except a projector such as is now prized as a museum exhibit, and a very few films of from 40 ft. to 60 ft. in length. Practical assistance or instruction was quite unobtainable. Anyone who had succeeded in making films guarded the process and the apparatus with the greatest secrecy.

As regards the films, so long as something moved the subject did not matter. To see waves dashing over rocks in a most natural way, to see a train arriving and people walking about as if alive was admitted to be very wonderful, but what was the good of it? All it seemed to be suitable for was to provide a "turn" at Music Hall, or a subject for a booth show at a fair, or an entertainment for children.

From the promoters of these entertainments grew the final demand for films. It should be remembered in criticizing the subjects produced at this time that they had to be such as would appeal to children or those in search of cheap entertainment.

It has to be remembered that the public up to this date had been accustomed to looking at lantern slides of exquisite photographic quality—single pictures upon which much time and skill had been spent. It was not easy to persuade people that photographs fit to look at could be produced by the yard by simply turning a handle, and many of the films shown at the time did not make it any easier. Then there were faults due to imperfect apparatus causing flicker and movement of the screen, and faults which were only gradually eliminated. The above is an attempt to describe the "atmosphere" in which the demand for films arose. Leaving out the early experimenters who although they never arrived at the producing stage are entitled to be honourably recorded elsewhere, it is

[1] By courtesy of Major T. Williamson.

interesting to observe that film producers were recruited largely from the engineering profession. Some of those made the production of films for sale their main object, and others the manufacture and sale of apparatus.

Brighton is often mentioned as the home of film production and there certainly were three different producers in this town about the time under review: Esme Collings, G. A. Smith, and the writer. Brighton also provided an attractive background and was often visited by producers from London and elsewhere, especially in later years. The three above mentioned will probably all admit that this coincidence and their early start were materially assisted by Mr. Alfred Darling, a clever engineer who made a study of the requirements of film producers. The writer at this time was floundering about with home-made apparatus and did succeed in making some pictures, but the real start was only made when the late W. Wrench, of Gray's Inn Road, introduced him to Darling. The Williamson Series of Short Comedies were not commenced until the year following the one under review.

Extracts from notes by Mr. Albany Ward, 1946, in a letter to the authors.

I was appointed principal operator to the Velograph Company, as well as working in printing and developing rooms by day and one of my first jobs was to exhibit pictures on the Syndicate halls at the Palace, Croydon, Metropolitan, Edgware Road, Tivoli and various other Syndicate halls as a Music Hall Turn. At that time on the Music Halls we showed from behind through a transparent screen, viz. a fine calico screen which was throughly damped with water and glycerine. This screen which was stretched on a frame which we travelled with us, and I well remember now, on one occasion, getting fearfully ticked off by Marie Lloyd, who was the Turn following us as we wetted the stage rather badly, to which she took very strong and forcible objection, particularly as far as language was concerned. I stayed with the Velograph Company for some months, during which time, after the Music Hall engagements, we toured the provinces with a special show which included the Diamond Jubilee pictures, and the programme was augmented with a vocalist and entertainer. We visited practically all the large towns, such as Birmingham, Manchester, etc., and I know we did a season at the Pavilion, Devonshire Park, Eastbourne, in the summer of 1897. . . . When I started on my own, with my own outfit, it must have been about 1898, and I decided to go touring, mainly in the West of England and in parts of Wales, and I think I was the first Showman to exhibit moving pictures to the bulk of the West of England, particularly Devon and Cornwall, where we certainly had a very fine reception, and for several years I made a point of going back regularly each year to these towns where I was given a great welcome. . . .

From the very commencement of my own Shows, I introduced sound effects with all principal films and found this a very great success. I had a film of a

Railway ride (*Phantom Ride* produced by Hepworth, I think) with a train passing through many cuttings and several tunnels. This gave great scope for effects and invariably brought the House down. Battle scenes, the Greco-Turkish War, Battle of Omdurman, etc., also gave good scope for effects, as did also Birt Acres' rough sea pictures, particularly with waves breaking right up to the camera and seeming to come into the audience, which created shrieks and real alarm in some cases. . . .

Early in the 1900's, a London syndicate run by Mr. Laurillard and several theatrical people opened up a number of sort of Shop Shows. Large shops, fitted with tip-up seats which ran about an hour's show, keeping open all day. These closed down fairly soon. Also about this time, Mr. Henry Iles started "Hales Tours" in Oxford Street. He fitted up a large shop like the interior of a Railway Carriage, the far end being the screen, and showed various films taken from the front or back of a train giving the effect of a train ride. He also opened a number of these shows in the larger provincial cities which ran for a year or two.

Soon after this, Ralph Pringle started to run pictures for periods of about four to six weeks at the principal cities and towns such as Free Trade Hall, Manchester, Curzon Hall, Birmingham, Floral Hall, Leicester, Colston Hall, Bristol, and ultimately Pringle opened several small permanent Cinemas in Bristol, but these were too small to face competition for long. Soon after Pringle's advent, the Andrew Brothers, Horace and Arthur, also started running long period picture shows at Plymouth, Portsmouth and some Midland towns and did well for a time. . . .

After leaving South Wales, I went touring again in the South-West of England and then decided that I would like to settle down and open up a permanent theatre, as I thought that a combination of pictures and variety might be a success, and I alighted upon a hall at Oxford in the Cowley Road which I opened on January 1, 1900 as the Empire Theatre, Oxford, which I ran mainly at the commencement with Pictures and Variety. At that time, one or two films had come on the market of a length of up to 100 ft. and these we regarded as star features. There was one produced by Georges Méliès of Paris, a trick film, *The Man in the Moon*,[1] which was particularly successful. Most of the films were however still short length, generally 60 to 80 ft. and were produced by Lumière and Méléis of Paris. R. W. Paul did quite a few, and I had a stock of films which I acquired from Mr. Acres, and also a series of the Velograph films who had done several good subjects, including the Nigger Minstrels on the sands at Eastbourne, Serpentello, a trick contortionist and several other similar films. Although I was settled in the Empire Theatre at Oxford, I still kept in touch with Pictures and went touring occasionally, exhibiting at various places in the South and West and also took a number of private engagements.

[1] *Sic.*

Filming the Grand National, by Fred Steele, written about 1932.

Staggered as I have been by the fortunes that have been won and lost on the Grand National, this topical event, on which the newsreel companies have gone all out, takes my mind back to the days when it was a laudable but remote ambition to have a film record of this classic race ready in time for exhibition in the main centres of population the same day.

It was just thirty-six years ago since I first handled a kinema projector, and, if my recollection serves me right, we were at that time putting on ten to fifteen minute shows of short films, not totalling more than 75 ft. as novelty interludes in the theatres and music-halls.

During our London tours we often played as many as six halls a night. The possession of a film, even if it was of indifferent quality, was such a novelty that it became almost a passport to the acquisition of worldly wealth.

It was all hurry and bustle, with a certain amount of thrill thrown in, packing projectors quickly and fumbling in and out of cabs—boneshakers, as we called them. The idea was two-fold—to make all we could while the going was good, and, secondly, to impress the people with our dash and verve in sparing no effort or expense to secure the immediate presentation of our epoch-making spools.

Adjectivally, the films in our own parlance were amongst the wonders of the world. One may well look back and laugh. Chances had to be taken, often with unexpected and queer results, in this mad and sensational haste to put over the films.

Once we happened to be playing in a hall in Liverpool during Grand National week, and the great idea was conceived of boosting a film of the race. True to tradition, cabs were ordered to carry the cameras to Aintree race-course; handles were turned. People were amazed. The plan succeeded beyond our fondest expectation.

Liverpool was billed with announcements that that evening a special race film would be screened, the idea being deftly suggested that our cameramen had been busy the day of the great race taking shots at Aintree.

In the evening we put on the picture of a steeplechase which had been sent to us from London. Unfortunately we had not run the film through before. Imagine our surprise, and also that of the audience, when we saw on the screen jockeys with side-whiskers!

The film proved later to be a record of a French steeple-chase, nothing like the National. You can guess the result. We got the "bird" that night with a vengeance.

Nowadays the exhibition of the Grand National film the same night in certain theatres is taken as a matter of course, but only a few people have any idea of the enormous organisation that is involved to achieve that result, or of the pioneering efforts of twenty or thirty years ago to make possible the results we achieve to-day.

Letter to the authors from Randall Williams,[1] 1946.

. . . There were at that time (i.e. 1896) my two brothers and myself. We were all professional photographers, which is how we came to be attached to the firm of Haydon and Urry, Ltd., of Islington. They were very clever scientific engineers but knew nothing about the photographic side. Between us we produced not only films but machines to show them and we really supplied 100 per cent. of the showmen.

The machine we started with—well, at that time it resembled a cheap sausage machine, but Haydon soon improved on that. We lost our reputation with it until the improved machine came to light. Then we lost our customers. They had all left us with head-, neck- and eye-ache. The price of admission was only 2d. So we had to find a way to get them back to see the show free, with a notice "For Educational Purposes." Well, then things improved as we had taken several local pictures around about Islington. Then they saw their friends, and their friends saw them which was undoubtedly marvellous. So to show our gratitude we put the price up to 3d. They then rushed the shop. We got less in our takings, anyhow we knew the pictures were going to take on, which they certainly did. The Police cautioned us about the obstruction and eventually closed us down.

The head-ache time I referred to was when our lighting system was an acetylene generator. Amongst the people inside the shop people used to hold their handkerchiefs to their noses and mouths. Otherwise we would have required a surgery for the patients. And the rude remarks they used to pass! Then we had the oxygen and hydrogen gas with limes—if we hadn't we would have lost our reputation again.

How new the business was at that time! We let the films travel on to the ground. And we had a row with the first person that trod on them. We ran them into a sack and wound them up after the show, which did not last long, as there were very few films to show (all in 75 ft. lengths)—such films as the heavy load of stone being hauled up a hill by six horses, the fight with the Sweep and the Miller, the Lady Overboard, and other films not worth mentioning which people would not be allowed to produce to-day.

Had we known then what we do to-day, we would have taken 75 ft. of film of the people coming out of the shop the first day or two. The facial expressions, and the rude remarks by the patrons of "how to get drunk without intoxicants," etc. They were right. It was nearly the beginning of the end of cinematography. Thank goodness the new Haydon and Urry machine and a free show just saved the position.

Off to the Fairs we went—terrific business everywhere! Then the small halls arrived, then the large ones, and then larger still as you see them to-day. Then

[1] See p. 37.

the travelling showman had to close down, and take or build halls where he could—that is where they are to-day. My first Fair to open with animated pictures was King's Lynn. So we thought we would arrange with the Dark Town fire brigade to turn out. Well, it was one of the hand pump types. It had to be hauled by two borrowed Cabhorses, which were all got ready for the "act," as it were, hours before. When our man knocked at the fire house door, on went the 75 ft. in a matter of seconds. After the pantomime fireman sent the horses back to their owners, a real fire actually broke out at a furniture shop, so we took our camera with another 75 ft. of film and photographed that. I think the fire engine arrived about an hour after as they had to go and borrow two more horses. I think it was at about that time, after people saw those local pictures, that animated pictures went up and never came down again. . . .

Screen Journalism

Like so many other aspects of the commercial cinema, film reviewing has its roots in the nineties. Criticism of a sort appeared naturally enough in the daily papers and in the press notices of music-hall shows in which the cinematograph was given its paragraph along with the other turns.

The final turn was that of Paul's Animatographe, which has proved so satisfactory to Empire patrons that one week's stay has not been found sufficient. As we have before stated the principle is the same as that of Trewey's Lumière Cinematographe, and the effect on Monday night was very fine. Among the pictures was one representing the Derby of this year, but the horses went past at such a rate that it was impossible to identify them. A street fight and the arrest of the offenders by the police caused some laughter, as also did a bathing scene at Brighton. The entry of a train into a station is a well-known picture, and was very well done, but the line must have been single or otherwise the train came to the wrong platform.—Extract from *Star*, Newport, Nov. 10, 1896.

As films became longer and the demand for them grew more constant, regular reviews appeared. The first number of the *Optical Lantern and Cinematograph Journal* in November 1904, contained a monthly feature called "New Films," in which each new production of the principal makers was summarized and appraised. Favourable reviews were used by exhibitors as publicity material in exactly the same way as they are to-day. Indeed, the general tone of the publicity of the time bears a striking resemblance to the lack of moderation in modern advertising campaigns, whose connection with the fair-ground barker has hardly been obscured by time.

The history of the first trade paper, in which the reviews, gossip columns, and editorial agitations on trade questions were already in full swing by 1905, needs some elucidation. The *Optical Magic Lantern Journal and Photographic Enlarger* was founded in 1889, and edited for thirteen years by John Hay Taylor. Animated photography became its especial concern from the article on W. Friese-Greene's experiments, in the June 21st issue of 1889, onwards. In March 1902, John Hay Taylor retired, and was succeeded as editor by Alfred H. Saunders. In November of the same year the name was altered slightly to *The Optical Lantern Journal and Photographic Journal*. Two years later, in November 1904, the first number of the *Optical Lantern and Cinematograph Journal* was published under the editorship of Theodore Brown.

The following account was given to the writers by the owner of the paper, E. T. Heron:

. . . In 1900 Hay Taylor edited the *Magic Lantern Journal*, which was the only magazine devoted to pictures on the screen, and reference was occasionally made to moving pictures. This magazine had been conducted successfully by Taylor for thirteen years. Articles were produced by Rev. T. Parkins, Edmund H. Wilkie of the Polytechnic, Professor Golding, J. Page Croft, T. C. Hepworth (who wrote *The Magic or Optical Lantern* and *The Book of the Lantern*), C. W. S. Crawley, Harry de Windt, Theodore Brown, J. W. Wright, Martin Duncan and many others.

I purchased the goodwill of the *Magic Lantern Journal* and in 1903 started the first journal devoted to the Phonograph, as it was called—*The Talking Machine News*. The end pages of this weekly were devoted to *The Cinematograph Chronicle*.

In 1905[1] I started *The Optical Lantern and Cinematograph Journal* under the editorship of Theodore Brown. In the opening editorial we prophesied that "home-made photo slides and living picture films would become as necessary adjuncts to future home life as the old oil lantern was in the past. . . . The demand for new films, a cheaper and improved form of projector and increased number of operators was evidence of a larger interest in the business. France had been the seat of the industry, although the living picture was born in England. A rosy future looms ahead for those who have laid the foundations for future business."

"Hints on Cinematograph Work" was the heading of a series of notes which made useful suggestions to manufacturers and operators. "Chats With Trade Leaders" included Charles Urban of the Charles Urban Trading Company, James H. White (Edison Manufacturing Company), A. C. Bromhead (Gaumont Company), and various heads of other firms. A series of articles "The Science of Animatography" by the Editor and an article on "The Flickerless Projection of Motion Pictures" were most useful in advancing knowledge of the practical work.

Towards the end of 1906 we decided to correct the name of Cinematography and in an editorial said in future we should start the word with K instead of C.

[1] *Sic.* November 1904.

We said "The Greek word Kinema (motion) and Kineo (to move) are the words from which motion pictures have received their title and Kinematics is the science of true motion irrespective of the force producing them." Our journal became *The Optical Lantern and Kinematograph Journal* and on May 16, 1907, I launched *The Kinematograph Weekly*. . . .

Specimen Reviews in *The Optical Lantern and Cinematograph Journal*.

"Another film these gentlemen" (i.e. Gaumont and Co.), "are selling is also very good, the title being *The Lost Child*. This is a film of the 'Chase' class, but the situations are extremely humorous, and at certain times exciting. The quality of the film is very good, each scene is snappy, and full of life, and causes a continuous roar of laughter."—February, 1905.

"Another film we saw at the same time, entitled *The Railway Tragedy*, is equally good. Whilst the picture was shown on the screen, our nerves were sorely tried. The scene where the lady who has been robbed in the railway carriage is thrown out of the carriage, and is seen lying on the four-foot way, to be rescued just in the nick of time before the up-express passes by, is a triumph in this particular branch of photography. The whole film is highly sensational, and we can recommend any exhibitor, looking for a film which will make the audience hold their breath, to purchase this film."—March, 1905.

"The Sheffield Photo Co. are coming out with a new subject called *The Life of Charles Peace*, and whilst it is a matter of regret that it should closely follow a film with a similar title issued by another firm,[1] these gentlemen inform us that they have been working on the subject for a considerable time, and that the scenes are original and totally distinct from the one already referred to. Officials who had charge of the case have been interviewed with the object of getting the details as correct as possible. The Banner Cross murder and Peace's sensational leap from the train were taken on the actual spots. By a strange coincidence the same engine driver was driving the train who conveyed Peace from London to Sheffield, when he made this sensational attempt to escape." —November, 1905.

[1] Walter Haggar & Sons.

Contemporary Forms of Sound and Colour Film.

It is appropriate to point out here that the colour and the sound films whose early history will be dealt with later when their eventual success is described, have been an ideal towards which film-makers have constantly striven, with partial success from time to time. Even in the period under review both colour and sound were occasionally used in some form or other, and experiments were frequent. Of course, the "dramatic describer" and the lady pianist were the prevailing answer to the need, widely felt for some sort of sound. But towards the end of the first ten years various systems of synchronized—or even unsynchronized—disc recording were coming on the market. These were, however, used exclusively for song accompaniments, rather than for dialogue.

Colour was present in various forms. Hand colouring was used by R. W. Paul as early as 1896, but the method was far too laborious to be at all widely used. The more usual practice was to use film stock tinted one colour all over—blue for night (e.g. Sheffield Photo Company's *Life of Charles Peace*—"the scenes of these incidents which occurred at night are artistically printed blue"), red for fire (fire scenes in James Williamson's *Fire*), and many other variations. The limitations of such a method are obvious, but its enormous popularity seems to have justified the higher price. At the same time, experimental projectors with filters and colour lenses were being tried out from time to time, and it was in 1906 that G. A. Smith patented his subsequently famous colour process, Kinemacolor. Toned stock was coming in towards the end of the period.

Film Catalogues Used, and Key Dates

The following film lists and catalogues have been used for reference:

CRICKS AND SHARP	Undated, about 1904.
L. GAUMONT	July, 1903
	May, 1904
	June 1904
	June 1904 (General)
	October 1904
	December, 1904
	Christmas 1904
	January 1905
	April and May 1905
	August 1905
	November 1905
	May 1906
CECIL HEPWORTH	1906 (General)
R. W. PAUL	August 1898
	September 1902 (General)
	April 1903
	July 1903
	April 1904
	September 1904
	Christmas 1905
	September 1906 (General)
SHEFFIELD PHOTO COMPANY	1905–6
	1906
G. A. SMITH	1898
CHARLES URBAN TRADING COMPANY	June 1902
	August 1903
	November 1903 (General)
	January 1904
	June 1905 (General)
JAMES WILLIAMSON	September 1899
	September 1902
WARWICK TRADING COMPANY	April 1901 (General)
	August 1901 (General)
	July—August 1902
	August 1902

In most of these catalogues, the films are either numbered or arranged. or both, in chronological order according to the date of publication. (Films which were made abroad and took some time to reach the main offices are therefore post-dated by some weeks, or even months). By ascertaining the dates of the topical subjects it is thus possible to date all other films, within limits of varying range. Further precision may be obtained from the dates of supplementary film lists, advertisements in the *Optical Magic Lantern Journal*, etc. The following key dates are assembled in this way.

L. Gaumont

3	July 1, 1902
15–17	August 9, 1902
42	October 25, 1902
50	January 1, 1903
54	February 17, 1903
79–81	May 11, 1903
109–117	July 1903
141–142	November 1903
197	by June 1904
265	by October 1904
278	by December 1904
288	by January 1905
294	by May 1905
335	by August 1905
374	by November 1905
447	by May 1906

From October 1904, there are also similar systems for Biograph and Clarendon films:

	Biograph	Clarendon
By October 1904		108
By January 1905	15	111
By May 1905	20	117
By August 1905		121
By November 1905		129
By May 1906	438	138

Cecil Hepworth

86	End of January 1900
108	1900
230	January 1901
275	March 7, 1902
333	August 9, 1902
369	February 7, 1903
394	February 17, 1903
485	June 1903
625	June 1904
731	February 1905
809	June 1905
994	February 1906

R. W. Paul

Paul's films are not numbered, but in the catalogues of 1902 (covering the years 1897–1902) and 1906 (1902–6) the films are arranged from back to front, i.e. 1906 in front, then 1905, etc. The order is not adhered to strictly, however, nor does it appear that the films are always arranged according to the same plan within the years.

Charles Urban Trading Company

The Urban catalogues contain several different series. 1,000 refers to Urban films, 2,000 to nature and 2,500 to microscope series, 3,000 to miscellaneous films and 3,500 to films of G. A. Smith, many of them taken over from the Warwick Trading Company. 4,000 refers to Williamson films.

1000	May 1, 1903
1053	June 25, 1903
1094	September 17, 1903
1148	by November 1903
1233	by January 1904
1246	by March 1904
1281	April 14, 1904
1294	June 2, 1904
1411	July 15, 1904
1502	February 4–12, 1905
1524	March 31, 1905
1527	April 15, 1905
1530	May 5, 1905

James Williamson

1–11	before September 1899
14–21	September 1899—January 1901
21a–39	before September 1899
41–56	September 1899—January 1901
57–88	before September 1899
93–123	September 1899—January 1901
124	January 1901
176	June 1902
194	August 1902
204	September 1902

Warwick Trading Company

5001	February 1898
5004–10	May 28, 1898
5164–5	January 14, 1899
5213	May 8, 1899
5537–42	July 17, 1899
5473	October 14, 1899
5482–3	November 11, 1899
5521	December 23, 1899
5536	January 23, 1900
5639–42	April 4, 1900
5678	May 12, 1900
5721	June 4, 1900
5727	July 14, 1900
5846–54	August 11, 1900
5866–71	October 29, 1900
5922	November 17, 1900
5957–65	January 25, 1901
5986–90	February 14, 1901
6045	March 29, 1901
6072	April 27, 1901
6151–53	May 31, 1901
6196	June 19, 1901
6247	July 26, 1901
6562	January 15, 1902
6610	March 22, 1902
6686	April 27, 1902
6697	May 30, 1902
6816	June 24, 1902

6898   July 19, 1902
6912–16 August 16, 1902
6919–25 September 3, 1902
7016–20 October 25, 1902

A considerable number of the films listed have been preserved by the National Film Library. Examples include:

Nursery (R. W. Paul).
Kiddies' Cake Walk (R. W. Paul).
The Human Flies (R. W. Paul).
A Chess Dispute (R. W. Paul).
An Accident Victim Revives (R. W. Paul).
Mr. Pecksniff Fetches the Doctor (R. W. Paul).
Persimmons' Derby 1896 (R. W. Paul).
The ? Motorist (R. W. Paul).
Gordon-Bennet Motor Race, 1903 (C. Hepworth).
Rescued by Rover (C. Hepworth).
A Reservist—Before and After the War (J. Williamson).
Fire! (J. Williamson).
The Big Swallow (J. Williamson).
Are You There? (J. Williamson).
Mixed Babies (Sheffield Photo Company).
The Miller and the Sweep (G. A. Smith).
The House that Jack Built (G. A. Smith.
A Desperate Poaching Affray (Gaumont).
Savage South Africa: Attack and Repulse (Urban).
Fire-Brigade Turn-Out (Urban).
Will Evans: Musical Eccentric (Urban).
Queen Victoria's Funeral (anon.).
Life of Charles Peace (W. Haggar).

BIBLIOGRAPHY

The main sources of biographical material are given in detail at the end of Part I, Chapter I. These include correspondence and interviews with many of the people concerned, and the proceedings (Numbers 21 and 38) of the British Kinematograph Society, being papers read on December 11, 1933 by Colonel A. C. Bromhead, and on February 3, 1936, by R. W. Paul, C. Hepworth, and W. G. Barker.

Material concerning the films themselves has been drawn almost entirely from such films as are still extant (e.g. in the collection of the National Film Library), and from the large collection of film catalogues listed in Appendix V. Reference has also been made to *The Optical Magic Lantern Journal* and its later form, *The Optical Lantern and Kinematograph Journal*.